THINGS MY CHILD LIKES TO DO

THINGS MY CHILD LIKES TO DO

ADMINISTRATION MANUAL

Joseph S. Renzulli | Jennifer Foreman | Laurel Brandon

Prufrock Press Inc.
Waco, Texas

Edited by Stephanie McCauley

Layout design by Raquel Trevino

ISBN-13: 978-1-61821-739-4

Printed in the United States of America.

Prufrock Press Inc.
P.O. Box 8813
Waco, TX 76714-8813
Phone: (800) 998-2208
Fax: (800) 240-0333
http://www.prufrock.com

Table of Contents

Introduction to Things My Child Likes to Do

A second-grade teacher might be surprised to find that, behind the missing teeth and cheerful smile, Tenille is reading at the eighth-grade level. Has she noticed that class clown Pedro can solve multiple-step multiplication and division problems in his head? She also may not be aware that quiet André spends several hours each evening polishing his cello technique rather than finishing his homework. Yet Tenille's mother knows that she has been reading voraciously since she turned 4, Pedro's parents remember how he used to carry a basket of magnetic numbers that were his "friends" all through preschool, and André's dad drives him to the nearest city every Saturday morning for his cello lessons.

Scholars continue to actively debate the nature of giftedness and talent, the means by which we should identify giftedness and talent, and the essential goals of gifted and talented education programming (Dai, 2010; Subotnik, Olszewski-Kubilius, & Worrell, 2011). Gifted behaviors emerge from the vast complexity of the human mind and develop continually as the interaction between heredity and the environment unfolds (Simonton, 2005). Meanwhile, administrators and teachers must make daily pragmatic decisions to provide appropriate levels of challenge and engagement for all students, including the most advanced ones (McBee, McCoach, Peters, & Matthews, 2012). Amidst this complexity, how can schools determine who is considered "gifted and talented," and how can they develop young people's gifts and talents to serve socially constructive ends? For gifted and talented educational programming to be defensible, it must logically flow from society's ideas about how to conceptualize giftedness and talent and how to identify those students who will benefit most from special programming opportunities, such as acceleration or enrichment options. Once certain students are identified, educators must determine which aspects of these young people's talents are most fruitful for developing with educational interventions.

Parents have a unique perspective on their children's behaviors, attitudes, and cognitive characteristics. Having shared experiences since their child's birth, parents can draw upon a vast repository of memories to form a nuanced picture of their children's strengths and interests. Moreover, parents know how these strengths and interests evolved over the course of development. This rich view of children's abilities makes parental input into educational planning essential. Things My Child Likes to Do is a tool that enables educators to draw upon parents' insights as they develop appropriate educational opportunities for students. This set of questions measures parents' perceptions of their children's display of gifted behaviors consistent with Renzulli's (2012) four-part theory of gifted education and talent development. This theory includes developing creativity, task commitment, positive character traits, and executive functions as elements of gifted behaviors that can be nurtured in educational settings (see Figure 1).

The original, 14-item version of Things My Child Likes to Do was written in 1979 and based on the learning, motivation, and creativity scales in the Scales for Rating the Behavioral Characteristics of Superior Students (Renzulli, Smith, White, Callahan, & Hartman, 1976). For this new version, 22 items with modern examples and additional content were prepared and reviewed by 203 professionals in the field of gifted education. Seventy-three percent of the reviewers were also parents. Reviewers selected the component of the Three-Ring Model of Giftedness (Renzulli, 1978) that the item most clearly measures (see Table 1). Reviewers were also asked for suggestions related to content coverage, item wording, and examples. Items with low rater agreement were removed, leaving 20 final items. Based on reviewer feedback, the following changes were made: Items and examples were revised or clarified, explicit comparison to age-peers was added to every item, and examples were physically separated from the items to more clearly show that the item, not the example, is what should be considered. This validation process has ensured that this new version is easier to use, more comprehensive, and reflects modern ways of interacting with knowledge and ideas (see Appendix A).

A VERY BRIEF HISTORY OF GENIUS, GIFTEDNESS, AND GIFTED EDUCATION

In the late 19th century, Francis Galton (1869/2006) proposed that genius was a function of a heritable, innate trait rather than being subject to external "nurture" factors. He also believed that the cognitive processes responsible for genius could be quantified through systematic measurement. At the turn of the 20th century, French psychologists developed the first standardized psychometric tests to measure human

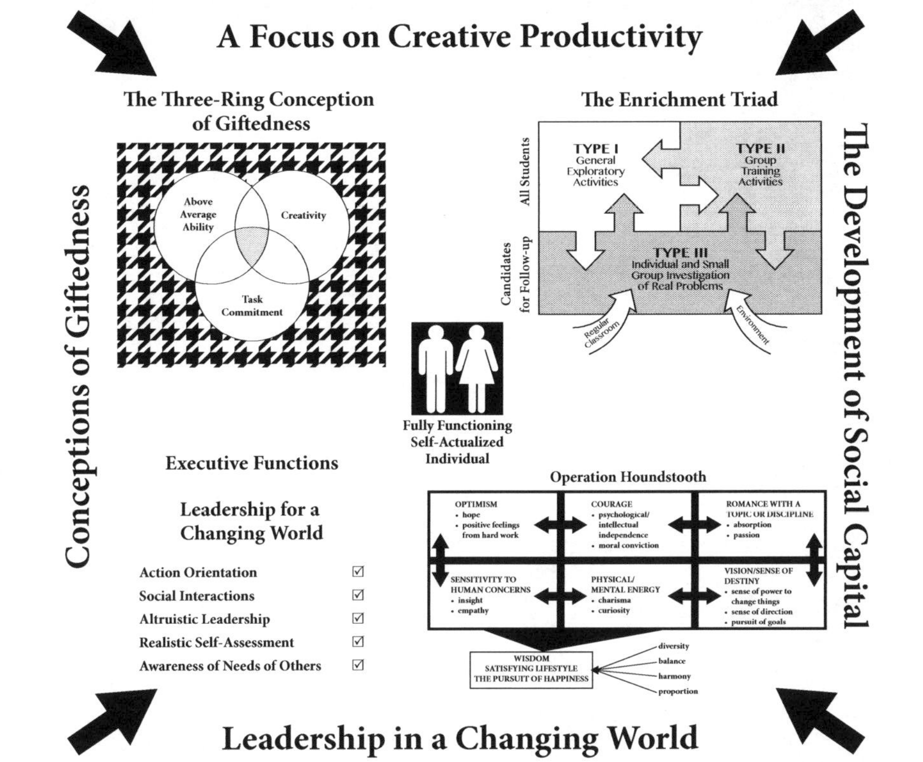

FIGURE 1. A four-part theory of talent development. From *Reflections on Gifted Education: Critical Works by Joseph S. Renzulli and Colleagues* (p. 36), edited by S. M. Reis, 2016, Waco, TX: Prufrock Press. Copyright 2016 by Prufrock Press. Reprinted with permission.

intelligence (Binet & Simon, 1905). Interestingly, these first authors of intelligence tests believed that human intelligence was a malleable trait that could be increased through appropriate curriculum and instruction. At about the same time, mathematicians (Pearson, 1896; Spearman, 1904) refined statistical methods that made it possible to assign a single numerical value (what we now know as an IQ score) based on an individual's responses to different intelligence test items.

Excited by these new methods for quantifying and ranking individuals' intelligence, U.S. psychologist Lewis Terman, having translated and adapted the French intelligence tests for an English-speaking audience, began research that equated genius or giftedness with statistically rare (top 1%–2%) high composite scores on standardized intelligence tests (Terman, 1926). Terman's seminal study followed 1,000 high-IQ children for nearly three decades to compare their outcomes with those of "non-gifted" individuals. Despite the eventual failure of Terman's studies to link high childhood intelligence test scores with lifetime eminence (Terman & Oden, 1959), educators of the early 20th century also began identifying students with high IQ

TABLE 1

Rater Agreement on Construct Measured by Each Item

Item (Example)	Intended Construct	% Selected Intended Construct	% Selected "None"
1. My child will spend more time and energy than his or her age-mates on a topic of his or her interest. (Joan is learning to program computers and spends every free minute writing code herself or reading about how to code on the Internet.)	Task Commitment	95.6	.5
2. My child is a "self-starter" who works well alone, needing few directions and little supervision. (After watching a YouTube video about musical instruments, Pedro began to make his own guitar from materials he found around the garage.)	Task Commitment	78.8	1
3. My child sets high personal goals and expects to see results from his or her work. (Marj insisted on building a robot from spare machine parts even though she knew nothing about engines or construction.)	Task Commitment	74.9	4.9
4. My child gets so involved with a project that he or she gives up other pleasures in order to work on it. (Donté is writing a book about his town's history and spends each night Googling historical records and documents—even when he knows he's missing his favorite TV show.)	Task Commitment	92.6	3
5. My child continues to work on a project even when faced with temporary defeats and slow results. (After building a model rocket, Sandra continued to try to launch it, despite several failures and "crash landings.")	Task Commitment	93.6	3.4
6. While working on a project (and when it is finished) my child knows which parts are good and which parts need improvement. (After building a scale model of a lunar city, Kenny realized that there weren't enough solar collectors to heat all the homes he had built.)	Above Average Ability	80.3	6.9
7. My child is a "doer" who begins a project and shows finished products of his or her work. (Maria began working on a puppet show 4 months ago. She has since built a stage and puppets and has written a script. Tomorrow she's presenting her play to the school talent show.)	Task Commitment	87.2	3.4

Note. Items used in this instrument were originally developed as *Things My Child Likes to Do* by James R. Delisle, 1979, University of Connecticut, which was derived and adapted from *Scales for Rating the Behavioral Characteristics of Superior Students* by J. S. Renzulli, R. K. Hartman, and C. M. Callahan, as appeared in "Teacher identification of superior students," Exceptional Children, 1971, 38, 211–214, 243–248.

TABLE 1. CONTINUED

Item (Example)	Intended Construct	% Selected Intended Construct	% Selected "None"
8. My child suggests imaginative ways of doing things, even if the suggestions are sometimes impractical. (Tracey suggested cleaning the refrigerator by moving it outside and hosing it down or taking it through the car wash.)	Creativity	95.1	3
9. When my child tells about something that is very unusual, he or she expresses him- or herself with elaborate gestures, pictures, or words. (Cameron compared the dancer's movements to the way subatomic particles experience a "quantum leap.")	Creativity	87.7	2
10. My child uses common materials in ways not typically expected. (Hunter proposed bringing a deck of cards when she went camping. She reasoned that if it was dry, her family could play Go Fish, and if it was wet, they could use the cards to help start the campfire.)	Creativity	91.1	5.4
11. My child avoids typical ways of doing things, choosing instead to find new ways to approach a problem or topic. (Mike had trouble moving a box to the other side of the garage, so he used broom handles as rollers and just pushed it along.)	Creativity	92.1	2
12. My child likes to "play with ideas," often making up situations that probably will not occur. (Keoni wondered what would happen if a scientist found a way to kill all insects and then went ahead and did it.)	Creativity	90.1	3.4
13. My child often finds humor in situations or events that are not obviously funny to most children his or her age. (Josh found it funny that his older sister lectured him on being more responsible and then got in trouble for leaving her cell phone on the school bus later that day.)	Creativity	49.8	12.3
14. My child prefers working or playing alone rather than doing something "just to go along with the gang." (Stephanie always misspells the first word in a spelling bee on purpose so she can sit down and do something she likes instead.)	Creativity	37.4	32
15. My child eagerly focuses on reading for an extended period of time. (Shawn stays up with a flashlight under the covers after bedtime to keep reading his library books; Sharif read the entire Harry Potter series over the 2 weeks of winter break.)	Task Commitment	74.9	7.4

Note. Items used in this instrument were originally developed as *Things My Child Likes to Do* by James R. Delisle, 1979, University of Connecticut, which was derived and adapted from *Scales for Rating the Behavioral Characteristics of Superior Students* by J. S. Renzulli, R. K. Hartman, and C. M. Callahan, as appeared in "Teacher identification of superior students," Exceptional Children, 1971, 38, 211–214, 243–248.

TABLE 1. CONTINUED

Item (Example)	Intended Construct	% Selected Intended Construct	% Selected "None"
16. My child pursues advanced reading material independently. (Marissa begs her parents to take her to the library every week and checks out titles from the young adult section; Lauren complains that her class is reading a kids' version of *A Midsummer Night's Dream* after she's already read the original Shakespeare play.)	Above-Average Ability	93.6	3
17. My child is eager to solve challenging mathematics problems. (Caleb accurately estimates what the total grocery bill will be while helping with the family's weekly shopping; Chris helps his older brother with his algebra homework.)	Above-Average Ability	91.6	3.9
18. My child enjoys challenging puzzles, games, and logic problems. (Leann solves the Sudoku puzzle in the newspaper for fun every day; Jackie can tell you from "in her head" how many inches are in a mile or how many seconds are in a year.)	Above-Average Ability	88.2	3.9
19. My child demonstrates curiosity about scientific processes and topics. (Samuel constantly asks how household appliances work; Devon always wants to go to the science museum on weekends.)	Above-Average Ability	74.9	7.4
20. My child reads about science-related topics in his or her free time. (Lakeesha always reads the *Scientific American* magazines while waiting in the doctor's office; Anna goes on Wikipedia and reads about new findings in astronomy on the weekends.)	Above-Average Ability	75.4	13.3
21. My child assists others with technology related problems. (Adam is the person everyone in the family goes to when they need a problem fixed with their computers, tablets, or smartphones; Alex helps his grandmother set up a Facebook account so she can see family pictures.)	Above-Average Ability	71.9	21.2
22. My child spends free time developing technology skills. (Jasmine has created her own website; Sierra has published several apps.)	Above-Average Ability	64.5	9.4

Note: n=207. Raters selected more than one construct for each item if they felt the item measured multiple constructs to any degree, or selected "none" if they felt an item did not measure any construct.

Note. Items used in this instrument were originally developed as *Things My Child Likes to Do* by James R. Delisle, 1979, University of Connecticut, which was derived and adapted from *Scales for Rating the Behavioral Characteristics of Superior Students* by J. S. Renzulli, R. K. Hartman, and C. M. Callahan, as appeared in "Teacher identification of superior students," Exceptional Children, 1971, 38, 211–214, 243–248.

scores for special programs with qualitatively different curricula. Early schools for "the gifted," like Leta Hollingworth's Speyer School in New York City, were founded on the Terman-inspired zeitgeist that giftedness was a stable and innate trait of individuals, which could be readily and reliably identified through scores on standardized psychometric tests of intelligence.

Over the past half-century, scholarly ideas about the fundamental nature of intelligence (Gardner, 1983; Sternberg & Kaufman, 2011) and giftedness (Shavinina, 2009; Sternberg & Davidson, 2005) have become increasingly complex and contextual. Although parsing out nuances in conceptions of giftedness may seem arcane and academic, the logic of how we actually identify and serve students in gifted and talented education programs should be consistent with our core philosophical beliefs about the nature of giftedness itself and how we come to recognize it in young people. In efforts to provide special services, schools often select and label students in ways that remain rooted in Lewis Terman's legacy: giftedness as an enduring quality of individuals that can best be measured by high scores on standardized psychometric tests of intelligence. We argue that this approach is not only unsupported by research (Brown et al., 2005), but it is also counterproductive to the efficient use of educational funds that could be used for programs to develop gifted behaviors in many students.

FROM GIFTED STUDENTS TO DEVELOPING GIFTED BEHAVIORS

Our belief is that giftedness is an emergent property rather than a static one, and that multiple factors beyond high psychometric intelligence—such as creativity, task commitment, and character traits—should be considered when choosing which students will be given special opportunities to pursue advanced and enriched school activities. We propose a shift in emphasis from the concept of *being* (or not being) *gifted and talented* to a concern for *developing gifted behaviors and talents* in students who have the highest potential to benefit from gifted and talented education services. This change in conceptualization implies that identification procedures should be flexible, dynamic, and ongoing, as well as draw upon a wide range of data from various sources, including teachers, parents, and even students themselves.

What types of gifted behaviors should educators strive to develop? Renzulli (1976, 1977) distinguished between two types of gifted behaviors: high-achieving and creative-productive. High-achieving gifted behaviors are generally manifested when students are able to efficiently learn and reproduce the types of information taught in the regular education curriculum, which often results in high scores on standardized achievement tests and high grades in school. Although this form of gifted behavior should also be nurtured, it typically does not lead to the production of new knowledge and products.

On the other hand, creative-productive gifted behaviors involve activities in which original ideas and products are purposefully designed to have an impact on one or more authentic audiences. Learning situations designed to promote creative-productive gifted behaviors emphasize the use and application of information and thinking processes in an integrated, inductive, and "real-world" problem-oriented manner. The role of the student is transformed from being a learner of prescribed lessons to a firsthand inquirer into problems of genuine meaning and interest. In other words, creative-productive gifted behaviors put young people's abilities to work on problems and areas of study that have personal relevance and that can be escalated to appropriately challenging levels of investigative activity. Because of society's need for individuals who will solve the unanticipated problems of tomorrow, special programs in schools should be designed to develop creative-productive gifted behaviors as well as high-achieving gifted behaviors.

Expanded ideas about developing gifted behaviors and talents have been incorporated not just in scholarly models, but also in applied definitions by education policymakers. The current United States federal government's definition of "gifted and talented" incorporates several of these ideas, including creativity and leadership, among the aspects of achievement that should be supported with special services in schools:

> The term "gifted and talented," when used with respect to students, children, and youth, means students, children, or youth who give evidence of high achievement capability in areas such as intellectual, creative, artistic, or leadership capacity, or in specific academic fields, and who need services or activities not ordinarily provided by the school in order to fully develop those capabilities. (U.S. Department of Education, 1993)

IDENTIFYING STUDENTS AT-PROMISE FOR DEVELOPING GIFTED BEHAVIORS

From a pragmatic standpoint, what types of measures would provide school decision-makers with valid "evidence" of these types of abilities? If we are convinced of the desirability of developing gifted behaviors and talents in a wider swath of young people than an exclusive, IQ-based conception would imply, we need more comprehensive, nuanced, ongoing, and even subjective forms of measurement to locate and serve students with authentic, engaging learning opportunities. We propose using an identification system that selects approximately 15% of the general student population for supplementary services (see Figure 2). In this way, both students manifesting high-achieving gifted behaviors and those who can develop creative-productive gifted behaviors can be identified.

Alternate pathways to identification would include parent nomination, for which Things My Child Likes to Do would provide information, as well as peer or self-nominations. Total Talent Portfolios (Purcell & Renzulli, 1998) can be used to compile multiple measures of students' abilities, interests, and learning preferences.

THE ROLE OF PARENTS IN TOTAL TALENT IDENTIFICATION

What role should parents play in determining which education opportunities are appropriate to develop gifted behaviors and talents? When identifying students with disabilities for special education services, federal law requires parental participation in the development of the individualized education program and selecting an educational placement that facilitates their child having a "free and appropriate public education" (U.S. Department of Education Administrative Code, 2010; U.S. Code, 2015). In these situations, it is customary to have parents complete rating forms documenting their children's behaviors as one component of the required multidisciplinary evaluation under the Individuals with Disabilities Education Act (2010). Although the Every Student Succeeds Act (2015) requires that states report scores of students at the highest levels of achievement and requires that districts receiving Title II funding must provide professional development on the identification and education of gifted and talented students, there is no federal mandate to identify or serve gifted and talented students with special programming. Accordingly, no broad legal requirement exists to seek parental input into decisions about what would constitute an appropriate education for developing gifted behaviors and talents. Therefore, parents' crucial voices may be missing from the information educators collect to determine how to serve these students.

What does the research say regarding the contribution of parent ratings to identifying and serving students likely to develop gifted behaviors? Numerous studies have documented that parents can accurately identify their children's giftedness (Ciha,

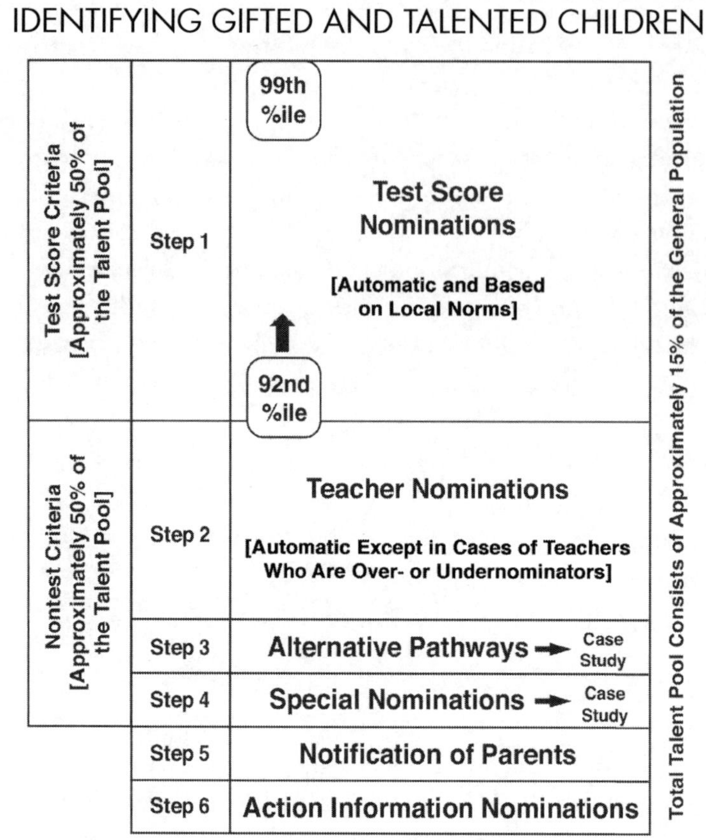

FIGURE 2. Nomination of Talent Pool students. From *The Revolving Door Identification Model*, by J. S. Renzulli, S. M. Reis, and L. H. Smith, 1981, Mansfield, CT: Creative Learning Press. Copyright 1981 by Creative Learning Press. Reprinted with permission.

Harris, Hoffman, & Potter, 1974; Karnes, Shwedel, & Kemp, 1985; Parkinson, 1990; Pletan, Robinson, Berninger, & Abbott, 1995; Silverman, Chitwood, & Waters, 1986), although these older studies have generally adopted a narrow IQ-based criterion for conceptualizing "true" giftedness. Hodge and Kemp (2000) found that parents of "potentially gifted" preschool students reported attributes of their children's behaviors consistent with the scholarly literature on characteristics of giftedness. The authors of this study noted: "Parents observe how their child behaves in everyday situations: interacting with adults and children, reacting to familiar and unfamiliar situations, and responding to difficulties. They know their child's interests and those situations that spark enthusiasm" (Hodge & Kemp, 2000). Things My Child Likes to Do is specifically designed to capture this critical information about the types of learning experiences that "spark enthusiasm," leading to long-term development of gifted behaviors and talents. The language of the cover letter for the rating scale is written in a way that seeks parent input about particular strength areas but does not place parents in the awkward position of favoring or jeopardizing their child's designation as a "gifted" student (see Appendix B).

In another small study (Hodge & Kemp, 2006), a majority of parents of young high-ability children thought that the teachers in an enrichment preschool program underestimated their children's academic abilities. Sankar-DeLeeuw (2002) found that parents of preschool children were much more likely than preschool and kindergarten teachers to respond that giftedness can and should be identified, and that early entrance to kindergarten and differentiated curricula should be considered. These two studies imply that parents' and educators' perceptions of young children's need for challenging and enriching learning opportunities are not always consistent, indicating that both sources of information are necessary to provide a holistic picture of children's educational needs. Although more research is necessary to determine how parents' perceptions of their children's behaviors fit into an inclusive model of developing gifted behaviors and talents, the available studies do indicate the value of obtaining parental input to contribute unique perspectives on young people's strengths, interests, and "sparks." It is important and ethically responsible for educators to make use of the results of this instrument, whether or not the child ultimately receives special services. This information should always be shared with classroom teachers and periodically monitored to determine if appropriate attention is given to information about special interests or activities.

CONCLUDING THOUGHTS

Things My Child Likes to Do is only one component in a comprehensive package of measures necessary for identifying a substantial proportion of young people who will become tomorrow's problem solvers. We believe that a more comprehensive approach to identifying students, as well as a focus on developing gifted behaviors rather than simply identifying "the gifted," creates a more defensible and meaningful approach to gifted and talented education. Parents and teachers must work together to nurture these gifted behaviors. The unique perspective that parents have on their child's strengths and interests should not be discounted or simply given "lip service," but should be recognized as a valuable source of information for targeting educational services.

How to Use This Instrument

The biggest challenge when using Things My Child Likes to Do is to inform parents that these rating scales have been designed to help teachers personalize their child's *overall school experience*. The instrument can certainly be used as *supplementary* information for making decisions about access to special programs or services; however, if parents believe that the instrument will be used as a major criterion for making gifted program admission decisions, they will feel awkward regarding their child's school options and opportunities.

The sample letter in Appendix B was designed to help with this challenge. The letter is worded in such a way that the gifted program is *not* mentioned in the letter. Teachers and administrators can modify the sample letter in any way they would like, but we recommend that the information being gathered not be framed in such a way as to be interpreted as a parent recommendation for the child's selection into a special program for the gifted.

It is suggested that (1) the instrument be sent to all parents (not just those whose children are being considered for the gifted program) annually at the beginning of the school year, and (2) each child's teachers receive the completed instruments. To maintain integrity to the stated purpose for gathering this information (personalizing their child's overall school experience), it is strongly recommended that teachers be provided with information about differentiating the regular curriculum whenever possible to accommodate particular strengths and interests that may be revealed through the use of this survey.

Appendix C provides a brief description of the various dimensions of differentiation that teachers should consider when making decisions about how to personalize the curriculum. Professional development on differentiation should be provided whenever a need for such training is deemed necessary. Most educational experts agree that all students should have general enrichment opportunities related to higher level thinking skills and strong areas of personal interest. Teachers who take advantage of special interests will undoubtedly promote greater enjoyment, engagement, and enthusiasm for learning on the parts of individual students, and the entire culture of a school can be improved when increased degrees of personalization and differentiation are infused into the regular classroom. Appendix D provides a description of how such infusion can take place.

The best way to interpret and use the data that emerges from Things My Child Likes to Do is to view it as information that tells us something about the student of which teachers may be unaware. Several important tasks should be completed once the rating scale information is obtained to follow up on any areas of strengths parents have identified. If parents have noted specific products or performances their children have created as examples of strengths, school team members might encourage students to bring in their products and describe them to school staff and/or fellow students. If their areas of strength are noted in performance areas such as music, students should be given the opportunity to give a performance that displays their area(s) of talent. After these "show and tell" sessions, teachers might interview children about their motivation to develop this product or performance (e.g., "How did you get this idea for writing a book about your family's history?"; "How did you become interested in building a rocket?"). Other questions should address the process (e.g., "What resources were used?"; "Did anyone help you?"; "How long did it take?"; "What were some of the biggest challenges?"). If parents are available, a follow-up phone conversation or e-mail can help establish more details by which the "validity" of a high-quality creative process and product can be determined. Interviews with both parents and students should be friendly and supportive rather than accusatory or critical.

If families are willing and able to submit tangible products as evidence of their children's motivation, creativity, and high abilities, teachers can make an additional evaluation of the level of performance exhibited in a student's work. Parents' enthusiasm about their child's work may be lovingly naïve and lacking in the comparative judgment that teachers (or other adults) have because of their exposure to the work of several students at particular age and grade levels. On the other hand, some parents may be more critical of their children's work and fail to recognize high-quality products and performances. In some cases (e.g., musical composition, computer coding, etc.) it may be necessary to obtain outside opinions about the originality or the level of sophistication embodied in a particular student product. Sometimes, faculty at nearby colleges or universities may be willing to provide expert opinions on excellence and creativity in these fields. Appendix E contains a research-based rating scale (Reis & Renzulli, 1991) that might be useful in guiding product evaluations, but it is always important to keep the child's age in mind when making judgments about the quality of students' work and to view the quality of this work in comparison to others of similar age or grade.

The third task to be addressed when using this instrument is to consider parent input in combination with (1) all other sources of data that are gathered to determine entrance to a gifted education program, and (2) the nature of the services upon which the program focuses. Any placement should always consider the best interest of the child and how he or she will "fit" in to the learning environment that characterized the program. Let us use an example of what might be a "bad fit" and a "good fit." Assume that a student named Liza with average grades and achievement test scores and mediocre teacher ratings has done a remarkable job developing a creative board game at home that her family and friends enjoy playing. Let us further assume that the special program is created to enhance an advanced curricular model that covers traditional subjects but at a faster pace and higher level of comprehension than the regular curriculum. Placing Liza in such a program might be a bad fit because her strengths are not compatible with the advanced curriculum that characterizes the special program. The information about Liza's interests and skills should, however, be brought to the attention of her teacher or some other resource person in the school or community. This activity lends credence to the statement made in the opening paragraph of the letter to parents:

> One of the major goals of our overall school program is to provide every student with an opportunity to develop his or her individual strengths and creative thinking abilities. We also would like to provide your child with an opportunity to do some work in an area of personal interest to him or her. In other words, we would like to supplement our basic curriculum with experiences that are interesting, challenging, and enjoyable to individual children.

On the other hand, the special program may be highly project-based and provide students with the opportunity to select their own projects and also work cooperatively with others with similar or complementary interests. Enrollment in that type of program would be a good fit for Liza, our board game designer, as the program might provide the opportunities, resources, and encouragement to further develop her board game, to explore enhancements, designs, and scoring options, and perhaps seek publication and marketing opportunities for her work. Services might include acquiring "how-to" books on game design, scheduling interviews with game designers or companies, and conducting field tests or a research project to gather data about age appropriateness, skill development, collaborative team versus individual competitions, or other variables that game designers typically examine when developing a new product. In contrast to programs that provide accelerated curriculum, "advanced" in this situation means services that focus on the enhancement of creativity, innovation and entrepreneurship, collaboration and executive function skills, and the development of self-efficacy.

As school team members examine the role of parent input from Things My Child Likes to Do, as well as all other information used in the identification process, it is important to remember *people, not instruments, make judgments* about the actions taken in any identification system. And above all other considerations, it must always be the best interests of the child that guide our decision-making process.

References

Binet, A., & Simon, T. (1905). New methods for the diagnosis of the intellectual level of subnormals. *L'année Psychologique, 12,* 191–244.

Brown, S. W., Renzulli, J. S., Gubbins, E. J., Zhang, W., Siegle, D., & Chen, C. H. (2005). Assumptions underlying the identification of gifted and talented students. *Gifted Child Quarterly, 49,* 68–79.

Ciha, T. E., Harris, R., Hoffman, C., & Potter, M. W. (1974). Parents as identifiers of giftedness, ignored but accurate. *Gifted Child Quarterly, 18,* 191–195. doi:10.1177/001698627401800318

Dai, D. Y. (2010). *The nature and nurture of giftedness: A new framework for understanding gifted education.* New York, NY: Teachers College Press.

Every Student Succeeds Act, 20 U.S. Code § 6301 *et seq.* (2015).

Galton, F. (2006). *Hereditary genius: An inquiry into its laws and consequences.* Amherst, NY: Prometheus Books. (Original work published 1869)

Gardner, H. (1983). *Frames of mind: The theory of multiple intelligences.* New York, NY: Basic Books.

Hodge, K. A., & Kemp, C. R. (2000). Exploring the nature of giftedness in preschool children. *Journal for the Education of the Gifted, 24*(1), 46–73. doi: 10.1177/016235320002400103

Hodge, K. A., & Kemp, C. R. (2006). Recognition of giftedness in the early years of school: Perspectives of teachers, parents, and children. *Journal for the Education of the Gifted, 30,* 164–204. doi: 10.4219/jeg-2006-259

Individuals with Disabilities Education Act, 20 U.S.C. § 1400 *et seq.* (2010).

Karnes, M. B., Shwedel, A. M., & Kemp, P. B. (1985). Maximizing the potential of the young gifted child. *Roeper Review, 7,* 204–209.

McBee, M. T., McCoach, D. B., Peters, S. J., & Matthews, M. S. (2012). The case for a schism: A commentary on Subotnik, Olszewski-Kubilius, and Worrell (2011). *Gifted Child Quarterly, 56,* 210–214. doi:10.1177/0016986212456075

Parkinson, M. L. (1990). Finding and serving gifted preschoolers. *Understanding Our Gifted, 2(5),* 1, 10–13.

Pearson, K. (1896). Mathematical contributions to the theory of evolution. III. Regression, heredity, and panmixia. *Philosophical Transactions of the Royal Society of London. Series A, Containing Papers of a Mathematical or Physical Character, 187,* 253–318.

Pletan, M. D., Robinson, N. M., Berninger, V. W., & Abbott, R. D. (1995). Parents' observations of kindergartners who are advanced in mathematical reasoning. *Journal for the Education of the Gifted, 19,* 30–44. doi: 10.1177/0162353295 01900103

Purcell, J. H., & Renzulli, J. S. (1998). *Total talent portfolio: A systematic plan to identify and nurture gifts and talents.* Mansfield, CT: Creative Learning Press.

Reis, S. M. (Ed.). (2016). *Reflections on gifted education: Critical works by Joseph S. Renzulli and colleagues.* Waco, TX: Prufrock Press.

Reis, S. M. & Renzulli, J. S. (1991). The assessment of creative products in programs for gifted and talented students. *Gifted Child Quarterly, 35,* 128–134. doi:10. 1177/001698629103500304

Renzulli, J. S. (1976). The Enrichment Triad Model: A guide for developing defensible programs for the gifted and talented (Part 1). *Gifted Child Quarterly, 20,* 303–326. doi:10.1177/001698627602000327

Renzulli, J. S. (1977). The Enrichment Triad Model: A guide for developing defensible programs for the gifted and talented (Part 2). *Gifted Child Quarterly, 21,* 227–233. doi:10.1177/001698627702100216

Renzulli, J. S. (1978). What makes giftedness? Re-examining a definition. *Phi Delta Kappan, 60,* 180–184, 261.

Renzulli, J. S. (2012). Reexamining the role of gifted education and talent development for the 21st century: A four-part theoretical approach. *Gifted Child Quarterly, 56,* 150–159. doi:10.1177/0016986212444901

Renzulli, J. S., Reis, S. M., & Smith, L. H. (1981). *The Revolving Door Identification Model.* Mansfield, CT: Creative Learning Press.

Renzulli, J. S., Smith L. H., White, A. J., Callahan, C. M., & Hartman, R. K. (1976). *Scales for rating the behavioral characteristics of superior students.* Mansfield Center, CT: Creative Learning Press.

Sankar-DeLeeuw, N. (2002). Case studies of gifted kindergarten children: Profiles of promise. *Roeper Review, 26,* 192–207. doi:10.1080/02783190409554270

Shavinina, L. V. (Ed.). (2009). *International handbook on giftedness.* New York, NY: Springer.

Silverman, L. K., Chitwood, D. G., & Waters, J. L. (1986). Young gifted children: Can parents identify giftedness? *Topics in Early Childhood Special Education, 6*(1), 23–38.

Simonton, D. K. (2005). Putting the gift back into giftedness: The genetics of talent development. *Gifted and Talented International, 21*(1), 15–18. doi:10.1080/153 32276.2005.11673053

Spearman, C. (1904). "General Intelligence," objectively determined and measured. *The American Journal of Psychology, 15,* 201–292. Retrieved from http://www.jstor.org/stable/1412107

Sternberg, R. J., & Davidson, J. E. (Eds.). (2005). *Conceptions of giftedness.* New York, NY: Cambridge University Press.

Sternberg, R. J., & Kaufman, S. B. (Eds.). (2011). *The Cambridge handbook of intelligence.* New York, NY: Cambridge University Press.

Subotnik, R. F., Olszewski-Kubilius, P., & Worrell, F. C. (2011). Rethinking giftedness and gifted education a proposed direction forward based on psychological science. *Psychological Science in the Public Interest, 12*(1), 3–54. doi: 10.1177/1529100611418056

Terman, L. M. (1926). *Mental and physical traits of a thousand gifted children.* Stanford, CA: Stanford University Press.

Terman, L. M., & Oden, M. (1959). *The gifted group at mid-life.* Stanford, CA: Stanford University Press.

United States Code, 20 U.S.C. § 1414(c)(1) (2015).

U.S. Department of Education. (1993). *National excellence: A case for developing America's talent.* Retrieved from http://files.eric.ed.gov/fulltext/ED359743.pdf

U.S. Department of Education Administrative Code, 34 C.F.R. § 300.305(a) (2010).

APPENDIX A
Things My Child Likes to Do

Things My Child Likes to Do

Joseph S. Renzulli / Jennifer Foreman / Laurel Brandon

Introduction

The items on the left-hand side of this document consist of some ways that children may behave. Examples are provided in the center column. Each example applies to a specific subject area or topic, but the item does not apply only to that topic. For instance, for Item 1, "My child will spend more time and energy than his or her age-mates on a topic of his or her interest," the given example involves computer coding, but it could also be *Joan wants to be a veterinarian and spends all of her free time reading about animal biology, volunteering at the animal shelter, and observing at the local vet's office* or *Joan is on a soccer team and voluntarily spends hours outside of team practice perfecting kicks and completing drills.* To save space, only one or two examples are provided for each item.

Directions

For each item, please indicate to what degree the item describes your child. Although you may not have had a chance to know many other children the same age as your son or daughter, your judgments should reflect what you think is typical for a child his or her age.

Item	Example	Not at all	Some	Much	If *Much* is selected, please provide an example from your child's life
1. My child will spend more time and energy than his or her age-mates on a topic of his or her interest.	*Joan is learning to program computers and spends every free minute writing code herself or reading about how to code on the Internet.*	☐	☐	☐	
2. My child suggests more imaginative ways of doing things than other children his or her age, even if the suggestions are sometimes impractical.	*Tracey suggested cleaning the refrigerator by moving it outside and hosing it down or taking it through the car wash.*	☐	☐	☐	
3. My child is more of a "self-starter" than other children his or her age. He or she works well alone, needing few directions and little supervision.	*After watching a YouTube video about musical instruments, Pedro began to make his own guitar from materials he found around the garage.*	☐	☐	☐	

Note. Items used in this instrument were originally developed as *Things My Child Likes to Do* by James R. Delisle, 1979, University of Connecticut, which was derived and adapted from *Scales for Rating the Behavioral Characteristics of Superior Students* by J. S. Renzulli, R. K. Hartman, and C. M. Callahan, as appeared in "Teacher identification of superior students," Exceptional Children, 1971, 38, 211–214, 243–248.

APPENDIX B

Sample Letter to Parents

To: Parents of Students in ______________________
From: ______________________
Subject: Things My Child Likes to Do

One of the major goals of our overall school program is to provide each student with an opportunity to develop his or her individual strengths and creative thinking abilities. We also would like to provide your child with an opportunity to do some work in an area of study that is of personal interest to him or her. In other words, we would like to supplement our basic curriculum with experiences that are interesting, challenging, and enjoyable to individual children. Although the work your child does in school gives us many opportunities to observe his or her strengths and interests, the activities that your child pursues at home can also help us find ways to enrich his or her school program. For this reason, we are asking you to complete the attached questionnaire and return it to us at your earliest convenience.

The attached questionnaire contains 20 items. Each of the items deals with a general type of interest or activity that you may or may not have seen in your child. The interests or activities might be the result of school assignments, extracurricular activities, club activities such as Girl Scouts or 4-H projects, or other activities in which your child has developed an interest. To help clarify the 20 items, we have also included at least one example for each. Please keep in mind that each example is included *only* to help clarify the meaning of the item and is not meant to restrict the item to the topic of the example. For instance, Item 1, "My child will spend more time and energy than his or her age-mates on a topic of his or her interest," includes an example about computer coding. The item is about time and energy, *not about computer coding*, so the example could just as easily be *Joan wants to be a veterinarian and spends all of her free time reading about animal biology, volunteering at the animal shelter, and observing at the local vet's office* or *Joan is on a soccer team and voluntarily spends hours outside of team practice perfecting kicks and completing drills*. To save space, only one or two examples are provided for each item.

As you consider each prompt, remember that you are rating your child on the 20 general items rather than the specific examples. It will, of course, be very helpful if you can jot down specific examples of your child's interests or activities in the right-hand column of the questionnaire.

If you should have any questions about this questionnaire, please contact the person whose name and telephone number are listed below. We very much appreciate your assistance in helping us to provide the best possible educational program for your child.

Sincerely,

____

APPENDIX C

The Five Dimensions of Differentiation

Sally M. Reis and Joseph S. Renzulli

"True differentiation requires that we look at all the characteristics of the learner in addition to achievement levels."

—Dr. Joseph Renzulli

"Differentiation is a journey that all teachers must take. With multiple levels of achievement, interests, readiness, learning, and product styles represented in each classroom, effective and meaningful differentiation may be the most important attribute of the 21st century teacher who wants to help each student make continuous progress in learning."

—Dr. Sally Reis

The diversity of skills, talents, and interests of students that we serve in our schools requires a remarkable range of teachers' skills, time, and resources. This brief article focuses on differentiation and the ways that teachers can adapt and differentiate the regular curriculum to meet the academic needs of all of their students. Challenges and solutions about how differentiation can be implemented will be discussed, as will a variety of strategies that can be used to differentiate, challenge, and engage all students. Defined simply, differentiation is matching a required curriculum with the learning styles, expression styles, interests, and abilities of students. It's predicated on the simple belief that engaged, motivated students score higher, are easier to manage, and enjoy learning more. Both research and current practice illustrate the importance of differentiated instruction for meeting every child's needs as well as raising achievement—and some of that research is summarized in this article.

DEFINING DIFFERENTIATION

In order to accommodate the needs of students across many different levels of academic achievement, teachers across the country have implemented within-classroom strategies referred to as differentiated instruction. Differentiation is an attempt to address the variation of learners in the classroom through multiple approaches that modify instruction and curriculum to match the individual needs of students (Renzulli, 1977; Tomlinson, 2001). Students vary in their abilities, interests, and prior knowledge. Differentiation serves to address this variation by matching the content, instruction, and assessment to students' needs and interests. Tomlinson (1995) emphasized that when teachers differentiate curriculum, they stop acting as dispensers of knowledge and serve as organizers of learning opportunities. Differentiation of instruction and curriculum suggests that students can be provided with materials and work of varied levels of difficulty, different levels of assistance, various types of grouping, as well as different environments in the classroom. In other words, differentiation is the opposite of a "one-size-fits-all curriculum."

FIVE DIMENSIONS OF DIFFERENTIATION

The three components that are most often associated with successful differentiation are curriculum or content (what is being taught), instruction or process (how it is being taught), and student product (tangible results produced based on students' interests and abilities), but more recently, Joseph Renzulli (1997) expanded these components in the "Five Dimensions of Differentiation," explained as five ways to integrate differentiation into teaching practices:

1. **Content:** Students have different academic abilities, and interests—and teachers can differentiate the content/curriculum delivered to their students. Some students need content that matches their interests, or is more or less challenging and appropriate for their reading level—and not every student should receive the same content in any given lesson.
2. **Instructional Strategies:** Students also arrive with different learning styles. Some learn best through group work and some by working alone; some learn best by doing projects, while other learn by discussion. Teachers can differentiate by using different instructional strategies that match the preferences of individuals or groups in your classroom.

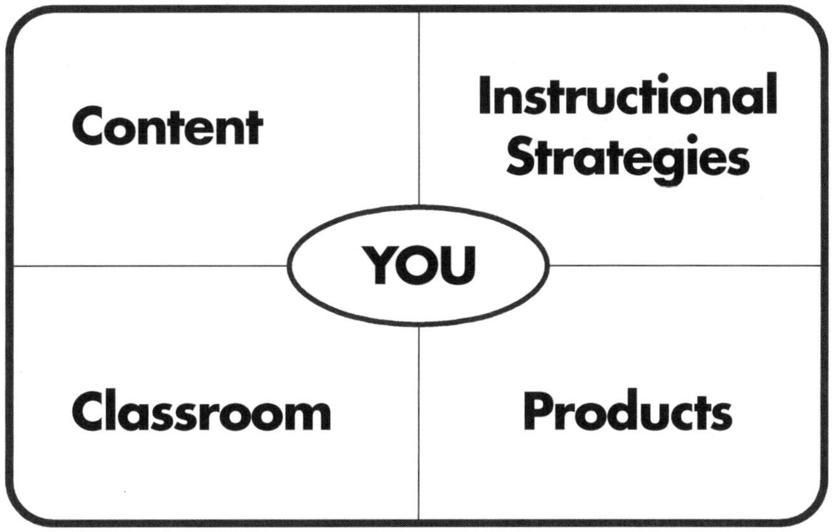

FIGURE C.1. The five dimensions of differentiation.

3. **The Classroom:** Teachers can differentiate the learning environment itself and how they manage it. Students can have the opportunity to work in groups with other students like themselves, or work in groups in which every student has a chance to demonstrate his or her different style. Or you can introduce new guest speakers or technology—or bring your class into new environments like the computer lab, library, or a field trip.
4. **Products:** Students express what they've learned in different ways—some students' preferred expression style is written, while others do better with technology, social action, or visually. Teachers can differentiate products by giving students options, when practical, to choose their own modes of expression to demonstrate what they have learned.
5. **The Teacher (You):** Obviously, it's hard to imagine that teachers can differentiate every lesson every day—so differentiation is about the decisions and choices that teachers make about how to differentiate the curriculum for a diverse group of students. Differentiation requires that teachers consider their students' learning styles, interests, abilities, and expression styles—and that they accept the freedom, flexibility, and creativity to implement this process in the classroom.

Renzulli's (1977, 1988; Renzulli & Reis, 1997) five dimensions of **content**, **process**, **products**, **classroom organization and management**, and **the teacher's own commitment to differentiate** provide a method to differentiate instruction. As noted in Figure C.1, the differentiation of **content** involves adding more depth to the curriculum by focusing on structures of knowledge, basic principles, functional concepts, and methods of inquiry in particular disciplines. Within the **content** area, representative topics are explored and webbed, with open-ended questions that probe into a particular field of knowledge (Renzulli, 1997).

The differentiation of **process** incorporates the use of various instructional strategies and materials to enhance and motivate various students' learning styles. The differentiation of **products** enhances students' communication skills by encouraging them to express themselves in a variety of ways. To differentiate **classroom management,** teachers can change the physical environment and grouping patterns they use in class and vary the allocation of time and resources for both groups and individuals. Classroom differentiation strategies can also be greatly enhanced by using the Internet in a variety of creative ways. The Internet can expand the **learning environment** far beyond the walls of the classroom and offers particular promise for engaging and differentiating content for children. Last, teachers can differentiate **themselves** by modeling the roles of athletic or drama coaches, stage or production managers, promotional agents, and academic advisers. All these roles differ qualitatively from the role of teacher-as-instructor. Teachers can also "inject" themselves into the material through a process called *artistic modification* (Renzulli, 1988). This process guides teachers in the sharing of direct, indirect, and vicarious experiences related to personal interests, travel experiences, collections, hobbies, and teachers' "extracurricular" involvements that can enhance content.

FIVE DIMENSIONS OF DIFFERENTIATION DESCRIBED IN A CLASSROOM

The following description illustrates what a differentiated classroom would look like if each of Renzulli's five dimensions were implemented. Content would be adjusted and changed to meet the needs of advanced students. In reading, for example, advanced self-selected reading materials would be used to challenge talented readers, and less-than-challenging but high-interest content would be used to engage struggling readers (Reis, McCoach, Little, Muller, & Kaniskan, 2011). Instructional strategies or **processes** used to teach and stimulate student problem solving and critical thinking would include, but not be limited to, problem-based learning, simulations, independent study (both guided and unguided), and higher level thinking questions. Higher level thinking questions should incorporate critical thinking skills to enable students to conduct research, brainstorm, identify problems and develop an action plan, and motivate students to pursue independent investigations of real-world problems—what Renzulli (1977) called Type III studies.

These types of **products** associated with a differentiated approach reflect both the learners' expression and the applied skills of a field of study. These products can be achieved through exposure to learning opportunities developed within the classroom or through the out-of-school environment, such as agencies, museums, TV, radio, community organizations, and mentorships or apprenticeships. When differentiation is occurring in a **classroom environment**, teachers use a combination of interest and learning centers across the classroom and organize study areas, computer stations, and work areas for products as well as artistic, literary, and scientific work. Some students will need to use additional out-of-school learning areas (e.g., library, gym, auditorium, lab) if the topic being investigated requires additional resources or environments that allow for freedom of movement. In the last dimension of differentiation, the **teacher** extends himself or herself by becoming part of the learning exploration through direct personal experiences, an opinion or belief that sparks a curiosity or confrontation with knowledge, or by modeling the love of learning. Using Renzulli's five dimensions of differentiation, educators can adapt and implement differentiation in a consistent and progressive manner to meet the needs of all learners.

DIFFERENTIATION BY COMPETENCY, GROUPING, AND USING COMPACTING

A recent emphasis on differentiated instruction calls for the use of assessment data to support modification of curriculum and instruction to respond to differences in students' readiness, interests, and learning profile (Renzulli, 1988; Tomlinson, 2001). Differentiated instruction emphasizes that learning is most effective when teachers are able to assess students' current levels of functioning and learning preferences, and then use this information to help students progress to more advanced levels of functioning and more advanced learning. This is exactly what the Renzulli Learning System (http://lpilearning.org/renzulli-learning-is-back) is developed to do. Renzulli Learning curriculum enables teachers to use data-based decision making to preassess student learning and use assessment, instruction, and data management to differentiate content.

Differentiated instruction combines flexible grouping of students with adjustments to the learning tasks; in some instances, whole-group instruction is the most appropriate delivery model, while in other instances, students work in small groups or individually to complete tasks that are targeted to their own levels of readiness, interests, and learning preferences. Kulik and Kulik (1984) studied the use of grouping—the practice of organizing classrooms in graded schools to combine children who are similar in ability—to ascertain whether there were positive or negative effects in their meta-analysis of 31 separate studies of grouping children at the elementary school level. The studies primarily focused on grouping students within a school into different classes based on differing average ability levels. After analyzing 28 separate studies that examined effects of grouping by achievement test performance, the authors found that grouping homogeneously rather than heterogeneously was more effective. Another study by Tieso (2005) found that significant student achievement gains resulted when teachers used flexible within-class ability grouping. To differentiate for students in homogeneous groups, teachers should use formal and informal assessment data to determine the most appropriate learning objectives and instructional strategies to better ensure that students will gain the most learning from being placed into these instructional groups. In addition to differentiating instruction for students in tiered groups, professional development for teachers, flexibility, and a combination of different grouping structures may also contribute to student achievement. In a 3-year longitudinal study, Gentry and Owen (1999) found that flexible cluster grouping had positive effects on all ability levels of students in a small rural Midwest elementary school when accompanied by professional development.

Another proven strategy for differentiation is curriculum compacting. Curriculum compacting, a service described by Joseph Renzulli and Sally Reis, is another process that can be used to eliminate or modify work that may already be mastered, and thus enable students to prove that they already know content. This strategy is one of the most widely used approaches to encourage curriculum differentiation (Reis & Renzulli, 1992). Curriculum compacting is an instructional technique that is specifically designed to make appropriate curricular adjustments for students in any curricular area and at any grade level. Essentially, the procedure involves (1) defining the goals and outcomes of a particular unit or segment of instruction, (2) determining and documenting which students have already mastered most or all of a specified set of learning outcomes, and (3) providing replacement strategies for material already mastered through the use of instructional options that enable a more challenging and productive use of the student's time. Curriculum compacting might best be thought of as *organized common sense,* because it simply recommends the natural pattern that teachers ordinarily would follow if they were individualizing instruction for each student. In research on compacting, approximately 40% to 50% of traditional classroom material was compacted for targeted students in one or more content areas. When teachers eliminated as much as 50% of regular curricular activities and materials for targeted students, no differences were observed in posttest achievement scores between treatment and control groups in math concepts, math computation, social studies, and spelling. In science, the students who had between 40% to 50% of their curriculum eliminated scored significantly higher on science achievement posttests than their peers in the control group. And students in group one, whose curriculum was specifically compacted in mathematics, scored significantly higher than their peers in the control group on the math concepts posttest (Reis, Westberg, Kulikowich, & Purcell, 1998).

DIFFERENTIATION WITH ENRICHMENT

Enrichment opportunities enable children to move beyond grade-level lessons and extend the regular curriculum with individualized opportunities. Examples of enrichment include exposure to new topics and ideas, training in creative and critical thinking skills, problem solving, firsthand investigative opportunities, the development of an independent study in areas of choice with individual research, and the use of advanced research methods. There are a variety of factors to consider when using enrichment to differentiate instruction and content. For example, what types of enrichment opportunities can and will be made available? Will the regular curriculum be extended with enrichment, or will it be compacted and replaced with teacher-selected advanced content? Will students have the opportunity to pursue their personal interests using independent study? Enrichment can take many forms, and these questions about content and how curriculum can be enriched are at the core of the decisions that guide enrichment selections.

The Triad Model, along with its larger-scale translation into the SEM (Renzulli, 1977; Renzulli & Reis, 1985, 1997, 2014), is one of the most popular approaches in enrichment education pedagogy (VanTassel-Baska & Brown, 2007), and it has been used with students in urban, suburban, and rural schools across the country with positive outcomes for the last three decades (Reis & Renzulli, 2003). The SEM has been used widely in both gifted and regular education programs, with this broad applicability of the SEM's three central goals: developing talents in all children, providing a broad range of advanced-level enrichment experiences for all students, and providing follow-up advanced learning opportunities for children based on interests. The SEM emphasizes engagement and the use of enjoyable and challenging learning experiences constructed around students' interests, learning styles, and product styles. Renzulli's Enrichment Triad Model and the subsequent Schoolwide Enrichment Model suggest the need for a comprehensive approach to elementary enrichment to differentiate instruction. The Enrichment Triad Model, an organizational and service delivery model, has three components: Type I enrichment (general exploratory experiences), Type II enrichment (group training activities), and Type III individual and small-group investigations of real problems. These models include elements such as enrichment planning teams, needs assessments, staff development, materials selection, and program evaluation.

In summary, classroom teachers can provide differentiated levels of enrichment to many students using various types of enrichment. Enrichment usually includes some or all of the following components: exposure to new topics and areas of interest, training in thinking and research skills, and opportunities for self-selected investigative activities of problems that students select or are assigned by their teachers. Enrichment usually includes emphasis on authentic content and process, enabling students to serve as firsthand inquirers, and exploring the structure and interconnectedness of knowledge. Enrichment teams, as advocated by Renzulli and Reis in the Schoolwide Enrichment Model, can help plan enrichment experiences for the entire school. Enrichment programs should evolve into an integral part of a differentiated system and should be regularly reviewed to determine both content effectiveness and appropriateness of delivery. All students benefit from a planned, articulated, and coordinated enrichment program that will provide differentiated challenges as well as engagement and enjoyment of learning.

DIFFERENTIATION USING RENZULLI LEARNING

The main goal of the Renzulli Learning System is to provide students with experiences that help them enjoy the *process* of learning through their personal engagement. Renzulli Learning is an online educational profile and matching database geared to enrichment resources, creative productivity, and high-end learning that matches student interests, learning styles, and expression styles with a vast array of educational activities and resources designed to enrich students' learning process. Using Renzulli Learning, students can explore, discover, learn, and create using the most current technology resources independently and in a safe environment.

Field (2009) studied the use of Renzulli Learning, an innovative online enrichment program based on the Enrichment Triad Model, for students in both an urban and suburban school. In this 16-week experimental study, both gifted and non-gifted students who participated in this enrichment program and used Renzulli Learning for 2–3 hours each week demonstrated significantly higher growth in reading comprehension than control group students who did not participate in the program. Students also demonstrated significantly higher growth in oral reading fluency and in social studies achievement than those students who did not participate (Field, 2009).

Teachers can use Renzulli Learning to differentiate instruction using four steps. The first step consists of a computer-based diagnostic assessment that creates a profile of each student's academic strengths, interests, learning styles, and preferred modes of expression. The online assessment, which takes about 30 minutes, results in a personalized profile that highlights individual student strengths and sets the stage for step two of the Renzulli Learning System. The profile serves as a compass for the second step, which is a differentiation search engine that examines thousands of resources that relate specifically to each student's profile. Student profiles can also be used to form groups of students who share common interests. A project management tool guides students and teachers to use specifically selected resources for assigned curricular activities, independent or small-group investigative projects, and a wide variety of challenging enrichment experiences. Another management tool enables teachers to form instructional groups and enrichment clusters based on interests and learning style preferences. Teachers have instant access to student profiles, all sites visited on the web, and the amount of time spent on each activity. Parents may also access their own child's profile and web activities. In order to promote parent involvement, we suggest that students actually work on some of their favorite activities with their parents.

Next, the differentiation search engine matches student strengths and interests to an enrichment database of 40,000 enrichment activities, materials, resources, and opportunities for further study that are grouped into the following categories: virtual field trips, real field trips, creativity training, critical thinking, projects and independent study, contests and competitions, websites, fiction and nonfiction books, summer programs, online activities, research skills, and high-interest videos and DVDs. These resources are not merely intended to inform students about new information or to occupy time surfing the web. Rather, they are used as vehicles to help students find and focus a problem or creative exploration of personal interest to pursue in greater depth. Many of the resources provide the methods of inquiry, advanced-level thinking and creative problem-solving skills, and investigative approaches. Students are guided toward the *application of knowledge* to the development of original research studies, creative projects, and action-oriented undertakings that put knowledge to work in personally meaningful areas of interest and provide students with suggestions for outlets and audiences for their creative products. The resources available in step two also provide students with opportunities to pursue advanced-level training in their strength areas and areas of personal interest.

The third part of Renzulli Learning for students is a project organization and management plan called The Wizard Project Maker. Using this project planner, teachers can help students target their web-based explorations to undertake original research, investigative projects, and the development of a wide variety of creative undertakings. The sophisticated software used in this tool automatically locates potentially relevant web-based resources that can be used in connection with the student's investigative activity. This management device is designed to fulfill the requirements of a Type III Enrichment experience, which is the highest level of enrichment described in our discussion of the Enrichment Triad Model. Specifically, the Project Maker provides students with the metacognitive skills to define a project and set a goal; identify and evaluate both the resources to which they have access and the resources they need (e.g. time, Internet sites, teacher or mentor assistance); prioritize and refine goals; balance the resources needed to meet multiple goals; learn from past actions, projecting future outcomes; and monitor progress, making necessary adjustments as a project unfolds. The Wizard Project Maker helps students make the best use of web resources, helps to focus their interests as they pursue advanced-level work, and establishes a creative and viable responsibility for teachers in their role as "the guide on the side." By helping students pursue advanced levels of challenge and engagement through the use of the Wizard Project Maker, we hope students will begin to regard their teachers as mentors rather than just as disseminators of knowledge.

The final step in the Renzulli Learning System is an automatic compilation and storage of all student activity from steps one, two, and three into an ongoing student record called the Total Talent Portfolio. A management tool allows students to evaluate each site visited and resource used. Students can complete a self-assessment of what they derived from the resource, and if they choose, they can store favorite activities and resources in their portfolio. This feature allows easy return access to ongoing work. The portfolio can be reviewed at any time by teachers and parents through the use of an access code, which allows teachers to give feedback and guidance to individual students and provides parents with information about students' work and opportunities for parental involvement. The Total Talent Portfolio will travel with students throughout their educational years to serve as a reminder of previous activities and creative accomplishments that they might want to include in college applications, and it is an ongoing record that can help students, teachers, guidance counselors, and parents make decisions about future educational and vocational plans.

Teacher resources in Renzulli Learning enable teachers to differentiate assignments, and send tiered and compacted assignments to students by placing them in their electronic talent portfolio. Teachers can also use Renzulli Learning to group students based on their interests, learning, and expression or product styles.

HOW MANY TEACHERS ACTUALLY DIFFERENTIATE?

Although most teachers, if asked, would indicate that they are committed to meeting students' individual needs, many teachers do not have background information to put this commitment into practice. Research demonstrates, for example, that many academically talented students receive little differentiation of curriculum and instruction and spend a great deal of time in school doing work that they have already mastered (Archambault et al., 1993; Reis et al., 1993; Westberg, Archambault, Dobyns, & Salvin, 1993). Many educators would like to adapt, modify, or differentiate the regular curriculum for their above-average students. Accomplishing this, however, is no small task. Too little time, too many curricular objectives, and poor organizational structures—all can take their toll on even the most dedicated professionals.

Tomlinson and Allan (2000) detailed the roots of differentiated instruction, as well as research relating to the importance of challenge in promoting engagement, growth, and authentic feelings of success for students (e.g., Csikszentmihalyi, Rathunde, & Whalen, 1993; Renzulli, 1977). Nevertheless, teachers still struggle to implement differentiated instruction, and among the challenges they face in implementing differentiation are concerns about planning for and managing differentiation, as well as fear of state assessments and little administrative support (Hertberg-Davis & Brighton, 2006; Katz, Stone, Carlisle, Corey, & Zeng, 2008; Moon, Brighton, & Callahan, 2003; Reis et al.,1993; VanTassel-Baska & Stambaugh, 2005).

With tools like Renzulli Learning, teachers have a much easier and more focused task of implementing differentiated instruction in the classroom.

GLOSSARY OF DIFFERENTIATION

Compacting—Determining goals of curriculum, assessing student mastery, and providing enrichment opportunities.

Differentiation—Matching the given content area with a student's interests, abilities, and learning styles through various instructional strategies.

Enrichment—Activities related to a student's curriculum or interest area that involve higher level thinking skills and guided problem solving.

Personalized Instruction—Customizing the curriculum to a student's achievement level, learning style, social-emotional concerns, interests, abilities, potential, creativity, and task commitment.

Instructional Style—Method of delivery used by teachers to stimulate learning within and beyond the classroom.

Modification—Changing the existing curriculum either by expanding the depth or breath of the content area.

REFERENCES

Archambault, F. A., Jr., Westberg, K. L., Brown, S. W., Hallmark, B. W., Emmons, C. L., & Zhang, W. (1993). *Regular classroom practices with gifted students: Results of a national survey of classroom teachers* (Research Monograph 93102). Storrs: University of Connecticut, The National Research Center on the Gifted and Talented.

Csikszentmihalyi, M., Rathunde, K., & Whalen, S. (1993). *Talented teenagers: The roots of success and failure*. Cambridge [England]; New York, NY: Cambridge University Press.

Field, G. (2009). The effects of the use of Renzulli Learning on student achievement in reading comprehension, reading fluency, social studies, and science. *International Journal of Emerging Technologies in Learning (iJET), 4*(1), 29–39. Retrieved from http://online-journals.org/i-jet/article/view/629

Gentry, M., & Owen, S. V. (1999). An investigation of the effects of total school flexible cluster grouping on identification, achievement, and classroom practices. *Gifted Child Quarterly, 43,* 224–243. doi:10.1177/001698629904300402

Hertberg-Davis, H. L., & Brighton, C. M. (2006). Support and sabotage: Principals' influence on middle school teachers' responses to differentiation. *Journal of Secondary Gifted Education, 17,* 90–102.

Katz, L. A., Stone, C. A., Carlisle, J. F., Corey, D. L., & Zeng, J. (2008). Initial progress of children identified with disabilities in Michigan's Reading First schools. *Exceptional Children, 74,* 235–256. doi:10.1177/001440290807400206

Kulik, J. A., & Kulik, C.-L. C. (1984). Effects of accelerated instruction on students. *Review of Educational Research, 54,* 409–425. Retrieved from http://www.jstor.org/stable/1170454

Moon, T. R., Brighton, C. M., & Callahan, C. M. (2003). State standardized testing programs: Friend or foe of gifted education? *Roeper Review, 25,* 49–60. doi:10.1080/02783190309554199

Reis, S. M., McCoach, D. B., Little, C. M., Muller, L. M., & Kaniskan, R. B. (2011). The effects of differentiated instruction and enrichment pedagogy on reading achievement in five elementary schools. *American Educational Research Journal, 48,* 462–501. doi:10.3102/0002831210382891

Reis, S. M., & Renzulli, J. S. (1992). Using curriculum compacting to challenge the above-average. *Educational Leadership, 50*(2), 51–57.

Reis, S. M., & Renzulli, J. S. (2003). Research related to the Schoolwide Enrichment Triad Model. *Gifted Education International 18*(1), 15–39. doi:10.1177/0261 42940301800104

Reis, S. M., Westberg, K. L., Kulikowich, J., Calliard, F., Hébert, T., Purcell, J., . . . Plucker, J. (1993). *Why not let high ability students start school in January? The curriculum compacting study* (RM93106). Storrs: University of Connecticut, The National Research Center on the Gifted and Talented.

Reis, S. M., Westberg, K. L., Kulikowich, J. M., & Purcell, J. H. (1998). Curriculum compacting and achievement test scores: What does the research say? *Gifted Child Quarterly, 42,* 123–129. doi:10.1177/001698629804200206

Renzulli, J. S. (1977). *The Enrichment Triad Model.* Mansfield Center, CT: Creative Learning Press.

Renzulli, J. S. (1988). The Multiple Menu Model for developing differentiated curriculum for the gifted and talented. *Gifted Child Quarterly, 32,* 298–309. doi:10.1177/001698628803200302

Renzulli, J. S. (1997, July). *Five dimensions of differentiation.* Keynote presentation at the 20th Annual Confratute Conference, Storrs, CT.

Renzulli, J. S., & Reis, S. M. (1985). *The Schoolwide Enrichment Model: A comprehensive plan for educational excellence.* Mansfield Center, CT: Creative Learning Press.

Renzulli, J. S., & Reis, S. M. (1997). *The Schoolwide Enrichment Model: A comprehensive plan for educational excellence* (2nd ed.). Mansfield Center, CT: Creative Learning Press.

Renzulli, J. S., & Reis, S. M. (2014). *The Schoolwide Enrichment Model: A how-to guide for talent development* (3rd ed.). Waco, TX: Prufrock Press.

Tieso, C. (2005). The effects of grouping practices and curricular adjustments on achievement. *Journal for the Education of the Gifted, 29,* 60–89. doi:10.1177/01 6235320502900104

Tomlinson, C. (2001). *How to differentiate instruction in mixed-ability classrooms* (2nd ed.). Alexandria, VA: Association for Supervision and Curriculum Development.

Tomlinson, C., & Allan, S. (2000). *Leadership for differentiating schools & classrooms.* Alexandria, VA: Association for Supervision and Curriculum Development.

Tomlinson, C. A. (1995). *How to differentiate instruction in mixed-ability classrooms.* Alexandria, VA: Association for Supervision and Curriculum Development.

VanTassel-Baska, J., & Brown, E. F. (2007). Toward best practice: An analysis of the efficacy of curriculum models in gifted education. *Gifted Child Quarterly, 51,* 342–358. doi:10.1177/0016986207306323

VanTassel-Baska, J., & Stambaugh, T. (2005). Challenges and possibilities for serving gifted learners in the regular classroom. *Theory Into Practice, 44,* 211–217. doi:10.1207/s15430421tip4403_5

Westberg, K. L., Archambault, F. X., Jr., Dobyns, S. M., & Salvin, T. J. (1993). *An observational study of instructional and curricular practices used with gifted and talented students in regular classrooms* (RM93104). Storrs: University of Connecticut, The National Research Center on the Gifted and Talented.

APPENDIX D

An Infusion-Based Approach to Enriching the Standards-Driven Curriculum[1]

Joseph S. Renzulli and Nicole Waicunas

The goal is excellence, always. And engagement in the task is the means to achieve it. —Nancie Atwell, 2015 Global Teacher of the Year

INTRODUCTION

One of the biggest challenges facing gifted education is how to balance the need to provide students with enrichment opportunities within the context of an overly prescribed or required curriculum. The emergence of standards in individual states and the new Common Core State Standards coupled with the almost overpowering influence of standardized testing has had the effect of squeezing highly engaging enrichment activities out of the curriculum. Many teachers have become so accustomed to requirements for "teaching-the-text" and overusing worksheets to grind up standardized test scores that they no longer have the opportunity or, in some cases, the know-how to deviate from prescribed material. Few would argue that standards-driven curriculum is not important; however, research has clearly and unequivocally shown that high-engagement enrichment experiences do in fact, contribute to higher achievement scores and they also make school more meaningful and enjoyable for students (Dotterer & Lowe, 2011; Greenwood, 1991; Reyes, Brackett, Rivers, White, & Salovey, 2012; Wang & Holcombe, 2010).

In this chapter we present a strategy that teachers can use for achieving some balance between the required curriculum and a way of infusing enrichment activities into standards driven material. Teachers who have used this technique have com-

1 *Note.* From *Reflections on Gifted Education: Critical Works by Joseph S. Renzulli and Colleagues* (pp. 411–426), by S. M. Reis (Ed.), 2016, Waco, TX: Prufrock Press. Copyright 2016 by Prufrock Press. Adapted with permission.

mented about how it has made them feel more creative about their teaching and more like professionals rather than mere purveyors of other people's material. Examples of exciting ideas developed by teachers are provided to illustrate how the technique has been used.

Q: How do bakers get the jelly in the jelly doughnut?
A: If you don't know the answer to this question, then take a look at the picture on page 53.

The Schoolwide Enrichment Model (SEM) uses an infusion-based approach to make prescribed curricular content more interesting and engaging. We do not criticize nor recommend "throwing out" basic curriculum, current practices, programs, or projects if they are currently producing positive results in both achievement and joyful learning. Rather, the SEM strikes a balance between traditional approaches to learning and approaches that promote thinking skills, hands-on learning, and creative productivity on the parts of all students. Our goals are to minimize boredom and "school turn-offs" and to improve achievement and creative productivity by infusing what we call the Three Es (Enjoyment, Engagement, and Enthusiasm for Learning) into the culture and atmosphere of a school. We can do this by placing an easy-to-use teaching strategy into the tool bags of teachers.

SELECTION, INJECTION, AND EXTENSION

An infusion-based approach simply means that teachers will:

- review and select highly engaging enrichment-based activities related to particular topics,
- inject them into the curriculum to make the topics more interesting, and
- provide support and encouragement for individuals and small groups who would like to extend their pursuit of the enrichment activities.

EXAMPLES OF INFUSION RELATED TO PRESCRIBED CURRICULAR STANDARDS

Two early childhood teachers in North Carolina collaborated to design a unit steeped in experiential learning that clearly meets the demands of numerous state and national standards.[2] They discovered that infusing the Three Es into the classroom allowed them to select highly engaging enrichment activities related to particular topics, inject them into the curriculum to make them more interesting, and provide support and encouragement for individuals and small groups who would like to extend their pursuit of the enrichment activities. The teachers in this particular unit of study for kindergarten social studies students in general education classes discovered that the Enrichment Triad Model could be infused into their unit of study entitled Global Explorations: A Multisensory, Multicultural Experience while meeting the North Carolina Essential Standards, the North Carolina Foundations for Early Learning, as well as the 2014 National Core Arts Standards, all listed below.

NORTH CAROLINA ESSENTIAL STANDARDS—KINDERGARTEN SOCIAL STUDIES

- K.C.1 Understand how individuals are similar and different.
- K.C.1.1 Explain similarities in self and others.
- K.C.1.2 Explain the elements of culture (how people speak, how people dress, foods they eat, etc.).

NORTH CAROLINA FOUNDATIONS FOR EARLY LEARNING

Developing a Sense of Self With Others

- Recognize, respect, and accept similarities and differences among people, including people with disabilities and those from varying cultures.

Social Connections

- Identify, value, and respect similarities and differences between themselves and others (gender, race, special needs, culture, language, history, and family structures).
- Demonstrate awareness of different cultures through exploration of customs and traditions, past and present.

2 We extend our thanks to Kelly Smith and her colleagues at Providence Day School and Gina Terry for sharing this example with us. We also thank Dr. Cindy Gilson for bringing it to our attention.

Creative Expression

- Participate in art, music, drama, movement, dance, and other creative experiences.
- Use a variety of materials and activities for sensory experiences, exploration, creative expression, and representation.
- Develop awareness of different musical instruments, rhythms, and tonal patterns.
- Imitate and recall tonal patterns, songs, rhythms, and rhymes.
- Respond through movement and dance to various patterns of beat and rhythm.

Motor Control

- Develop small muscle control and coordination.
- Experiment with hand-held tools that develop strength, control, and dexterity of small muscles (e.g., spoons, paintbrushes, crayons, markers, safety scissors, and a variety of technological tools, with adaptations as needed).
- Increase the ability to move their bodies in space (running, jumping, spinning).

2014 NATIONAL CORE ARTS STANDARDS

- MU:Cr.1.1PreKa With substantial guidance, explore and experience a variety of music.
- MU:Cr2.1.PREKa With substantial guidance, explore favorite musical ideas (such as movements, vocalizations, or instrumental accompaniments).
- Visual Standards: Relate artistic ideas and works with societal, cultural and historical context to deepen understanding.
- VA:Cn11.1.1a Understand that people from different places and times have made art for a variety of reasons.
- Dance DA:Cn11.1.1:a Watch and/or perform a dance from a different culture and discuss or demonstrate the types of movement danced.

The SEM, and in particular, the Enrichment Triad Model, provided these teachers with the tools that they needed in order to master each of the standards that North Carolina set forth. The students became engaged in the opportunity to explore three different countries during an integrated, month-long unit of study. Three separate classrooms were dedicated to this unit, each focusing on one of three countries—Greece, Brazil, and Japan—and the students spent one week in each. The exploration in each classroom was rich in details of the culture of each country, with a focus on arts, language, traditions, music, movement, and food. Each classroom had a combination of small-group learning centers where students could explore individual and small-group interests, as well as whole-class lessons. In addition, prior to their journeys, the children created their own "passports" and "suitcases" and then spent their final days preparing to present what they had learned and discovered, based on their interests, to their parents during a Global Day celebration.

TYPE I ENRICHMENT

The teachers planned ahead by preparing many Type I activities, including websites and DVDs showing images, customs, and traditional celebrations (dances) from each country, as well as children's books (both fictional and reference) for students to explore including individual countries, travel, world, global citizenship, among others. Speakers were invited into classrooms, including the music teacher, dance teacher, travel agents, and presenters who had visited or lived in one of the countries. Globes and maps, instruments and recordings of traditional music, artifacts from countries for display and student exploration were located in each room. In addition, each classroom had Interest Development Centers that held a wide variety of materials and activities that engaged the students and stimulated their individual curiosities. Students toured these "countries" and carried "I Wonder" charts upon which they could write down their questions and ideas. At the end of each opportunity to be in a "country" classroom, the students gathered together with their charts to talk about what they had experienced during the day's "tour." The teacher would follow up with the students by asking:

- What did you learn about today?
- What did you find exciting or interesting?
- Do you have anything to add to the "I Wonder" chart today?

As the teachers moved from these Type I activities into Type II methodology, they had some important questions to ask themselves, and they needed to keep the standards in mind. During the Type I activities, the students had the opportunity to see and question the differences between themselves and other cultures and begin to dig more deeply into what they had discovered. To engage in Type II Enrichment, the students became active thinkers and the teachers became the trainers, facilitators, and discussion leaders (Maker & Schiever, 2005), what we sometimes refer to as the "guide-on-the-side."

There were some important questions that would help to guide the teachers in this enrichment effort and enable them to continue to meet the standards. Infusion of Type II Enrichment allowed for the teacher to meet the standards and keep students engaged in the work.

TYPE II ENRICHMENT

Type II Enrichment includes both materials and methods that promote the development of thinking and feeling processes. Some Type II training is general and some is specific. Type II Enrichment is usually conducted in classrooms and enrichment programs and includes the development of: (1) creative thinking and problem solving, critical thinking, and affective processes; (2) a wide variety of specific learning how-to-learn skills; (3) skills in the appropriate use of advanced-level reference materials; and (4) written, oral, and visual communication skills. Other Type II Enrichment is specific, as it cannot be planned in advance and usually involves advanced methodological instruction in an area of interest selected by the student. The unit creators thought about the following as they developed the Type II Enrichment:

What prior knowledge should students have to complete this lesson?

- Students will have introductory information about the three countries from Type I activities.
- Students will complete a brainstorming activity with the "I Wonder" chart.

What content or skills will students learn?

- Students will develop skills in the following domains: social, fine motor, gross motor, visual art, musical, aural, spatial awareness, language, writing, emergent reading, creative problem solving, and mathematical.
- Students will gain information in the following content areas: social studies (history, geography, cultural awareness), technology, music, visual art, dance, culinary arts, and foreign language.

How will you model the Type II Enrichment content or skills?

- The teacher will model the appropriate thinking and feeling processes during interactions with students by brainstorming, hypothesizing, making observations, and offering interpretations of data . . . in a minimal, but guiding way.

Describe any activities related to guided and independent practice.

- Each learning center will have activities with guided practice and completed examples where appropriate.

List at least three examples of open-ended questions that you will ask students during the Type II Enrichment experience.

- Analysis—Compare and contrast elements of each culture: How are the dances similar? How are the languages and alphabet different?
- Evaluation—Assess experiences: What were your favorite/least favorite food samples? What art project did you enjoy the most/least?
- Interpretation—What part of the culture is most like your own?
- Hypothesizing—How do you think your life would be different if you were growing up in one of the other countries?

How will you assess student mastery of the Type II content or skills?

- Students will complete a follow up to the group's "I Wonder" chart entitled "Now I Know" through the process of a brief individual interview.

How will you add closure to your lessons?

- Have students identify and share which Type II process skills were learned and utilized at the end of each day.
- "Global Day" will showcase products and activities from learning centers.

Once the teachers took the time to infuse Type II Enrichment into the monthlong integrated unit on different cultures, which would culminate in Global Day, showcasing their accomplishments for an authentic audience, they could see how many standards had been mastered through Type I and Type II activities and how they could utilize Type III Enrichment in order to enable students to finish their projects and complete the list of standards that remained.

TYPE III ENRICHMENT

In Type III, the students assume the role of the problem finder, data gatherer, producer, and inquirer and the teacher took on the role of the manager and became a resource for students. The unit creators asked themselves:

- What will students do at this stage? Where will they work on their projects?
- What will your role be during this stage?
- How will you assess students' Type III Enrichment?
- How will students share their Type III Enrichment with a real-world audience?

As the students dove into Type III Enrichment, the teacher's role turned to helping to identify and refine student interests, to find an appropriate outlet for their products, to develop a laboratory environment, and to provide pedagogical assistance (Maker & Schiever, 2005).

As the students geared up to work on refining their interests and discovering the best way to showcase their work, there were specific goals and resources that had to be identified:

- General interests of students must be refined and focused.
- Students must identify a real problem that can be solved.
- Students must apply proper investigative strategies.
- Students must be allowed to make their own decisions.

In addition, the unit creators asked themselves, "Where will students work on their projects?":

- In the classroom
- In the outdoor classroom (particularly if the investigation is related to nature)

- Research can be conducted in the music room if the investigation is related to music
- In the art room, if more resources are necessary
- *It all depends on where student interests lead and what type of research is necessary* (Smith & Terry, 2014).

Based on areas of interest, possible Type III projects included: presentations; designing a brochure; taking a poll of a favorite food or place; creating an advertisement or TV show; creating an interpretive dance or song; creating a short story or skit from the perspective of a child living in said country; sharing a library or personally owned book about one of the countries; expanding learning stations to include an area not part of the lesson (such as indigenous animals, unique consumer products, popular sports, famous figures); creating a photo scrapbook of the classmates' experiences as they visit each room; and constructing a diorama of a landmark or other scene from a country.

Students were assessed on their "level of readiness and interest in presenting to visitors on Global Day" (Smith & Terry, 2014). In addition, they had opportunities to prepare to showcase their findings to their fellow classmates and teachers prior to Global Day. On the final day of presentations, those students who participated in Type III Enrichment presented their problem (what they researched), the solution (what they discovered), and their product (what they created) to their audience. Those students who did not complete a Type III product were stationed at various learning centers to provide information about what was located at each. In this manner, all students, from those who were able to complete a Type III investigation to those who were not, had the opportunity to present, even if at different levels of understanding.

The following less formal but equally demonstrative examples show how an infusion-based enrichment approach works in various subject areas.

- An elementary teacher was required to have her students memorize all the states and capitals of U.S. cities. To make the assignment more interesting, she gave them an opportunity to select a project that had something to do with this topic and that was related to a personal interest. One group of students interested in music decided to develop a rap song for their state's official anthem. Another group interested in history decided to develop historic site maps, posters, and travel brochures for a state they had visited or would like to visit some day. A third group used state-shaped cookie cutters to make an edible map of the U.S. using chocolate bits to designate the locations of each state's capital. This group of students was so enthusiastic that they extended their work by visiting other classrooms, sharing their cookies with other classes, and providing brief historical facts about some of the states.
- A middle-grade math teacher had her students develop fictional fantasy baseball cards and analyze the players' statistics to draft and trade players while

building their own teams. They drew caricatures of their players and a "Player Wheel" with geometric representations of players' strengths and weaknesses was created and used to play against other students' teams. A regular season schedule was set for the class, ending with a World Series game to decide the classroom champion.

- A high school AP Physics teacher assigned a yearlong project that encouraged students to use all of the concepts they covered in his course for addressing a practical problem. The project asked students to apply everything they had learned in physics. One group decided to study the topography of their area by launching a weather balloon carrying a video camera, a GPS tracking device, and various weather data-gathering instruments high above the Earth's surface. They recorded the journey, prepared topographical maps, and analyzed data about temperature, air pressure, and humidity. At the end of each unit of study, the teacher asked students how the principles and concepts they studied in the unit applied to their project, making learning more relevant and meaningful.
- A middle school social studies teacher covering Ancient Egypt used the GoQuest database to find a site that enabled students to conduct a virtual dissection and preservation of their own mummies. Tools for removing organs, labeling them, placing them in jars, and glueing, wrapping, and preserving their mummies enabled them to have hands-on experiences that made this topic more meaningful. Material in hypertext familiarized the students with Egyptian language and culture. The excitement of this activity created far-reaching affects on interest and motivation that extended beyond simply covering the material in a textbook.

THE ROLE OF TECHNOLOGY IN FINDING RESOURCES FOR INFUSION

This engagement and infusion approach works because teachers have the tools to implant highly engaging material into the standards based curriculum and to use technology to locate what we call Just-In-Time (J-I-T) knowledge that is relevant to their projects—exactly what adult researchers do as they go about the investigative and creative processes. The advent and easy access to the larger world of knowledge has provided opportunities to make formal learning a different process than it was a decade or two ago. Today's young people are digital learners and emerging masters of interactive media technology using cell phones and handheld devices regularly to access J-I-T information (e.g., movie, bus, and TV schedules, sports scores, restaurants, etc.).

Traditional ways of learning, even under the best of circumstances, cannot compete with students who find texting under their desks more engaging than listening to their teachers and professors or memorizing factual material for a forthcoming test.

Another development in technology that will aid infusion is the unlimited amount of information now available through the Internet. Thousands of free course-related materials are easily accessible through organizations such as the Khan Academy, which has produced more than 4,000 videos on topics across all grade levels and several curricular areas. The Massive Open Online Courses sponsored by some of the best-known universities in the country, including MIT's OpenCourseWare program and Coursera, have produced thousands of courses that can be widely accessed without cost.

Changing the learning process has become a reality due to the unlimited access to the knowledge sources mentioned above. Teachers, however, can also become creative contributors to the resource stockpile and the producers of their own televised lectures, course-related material, and media events. Free or inexpensive software now enables teachers to prepare and upload their own lectures and assignments for student use anytime and anywhere through the application of easy-to-use screen casting software (e.g., Camtasia Studio 8, Screenflow Software).

A program called Juno (http://gofrontrow.com/en/juno) enables easy recording of high-quality audio/video clips without adding any extra work to a teacher's day. The program automatically adds titles and prepares files for uploading that can then be accessed by computers, tablets, smartphones, or interactive white boards. In addition, as mentioned above, content recorded by others is readily available in all subject areas. These resources enable teachers to easily turn their lectures and related lesson planning tools into audio and video podcasts and printed course and video materials that can then be uploaded for student access. We can capitalize on students' fascination and skills with technology and the availability of vast amounts of online material by giving teachers the license and ability to infuse creativity and thinking skills activities into standards driven curriculum.

Although it is not practical to use infusion for every topic or course, this approach makes learning more engaging and creates an enthusiasm for learning that seldom results from covering curricular material in traditional ways. The guidelines for infusion are easy to follow:

- Select an activity that does not always have a single, predetermined correct answer.
- Find things that students do rather than sit and listen to.
- Give students choices that they will enjoy pursuing.
- Select activities that have various levels of challenge to which interested students can escalate.

Finding activities for infusion is now easier than ever. Internet-based search engines allow teachers to enter topics, subtopics, and sub-subtopics by subject area, grade level, and difficulty level. Thousands of high-engagement activities that enable teachers to locate and infuse an almost endless array of exciting enrichment activities can be found with this new technology.

PREPARING FOR THE INFUSION PROCESS

In the example mentioned above related to learning the names of U.S. states and capitals, teachers used infusion activities in order to engage students' enthusiasm for learning. A traditional brainstorming technique[3] and the Creative Idea Generator presented in Figure D.1 were infused into the lesson in order to engage students to come up with as many ideas as possible for making the teaching of this topic more interesting. Guidelines for brainstorming were briefly discussed and teachers were asked to apply as many of the following criteria as possible to the brainstorming process.

1. The activity has a relationship to one or more regular curriculum topics.
2. There is not a single, predetermined correct answer or solution to the problem raised in the activity.
3. The activity consists of something students do rather than sit and listen to.
4. The activity is fun for most students.
5. The activity should lead to some form of product development on the parts of students.
6. The activity has various levels of challenge to which interested students can escalate if they would like to creatively extend the interest through follow-up activity.

Students were then given an opportunity to select an activity that they would like to pursue based on their individual interests and learning styles. Most students chose to work in groups, however a few students preferred to work on their own. Infusion activities cannot only make a traditional, memory-oriented topic more interesting, they can also present opportunities for developing creative, analytic, and investigative learning skills. Students learn cooperative, collaborative, and other executive function skills, strategies for acquiring J-I-T information, and most importantly, that learning is, in and of itself, an enjoyable process.

3 Brainstorming is a group or individual creativity technique by which efforts are made to spontaneously list many ideas for addressing a particular problem.

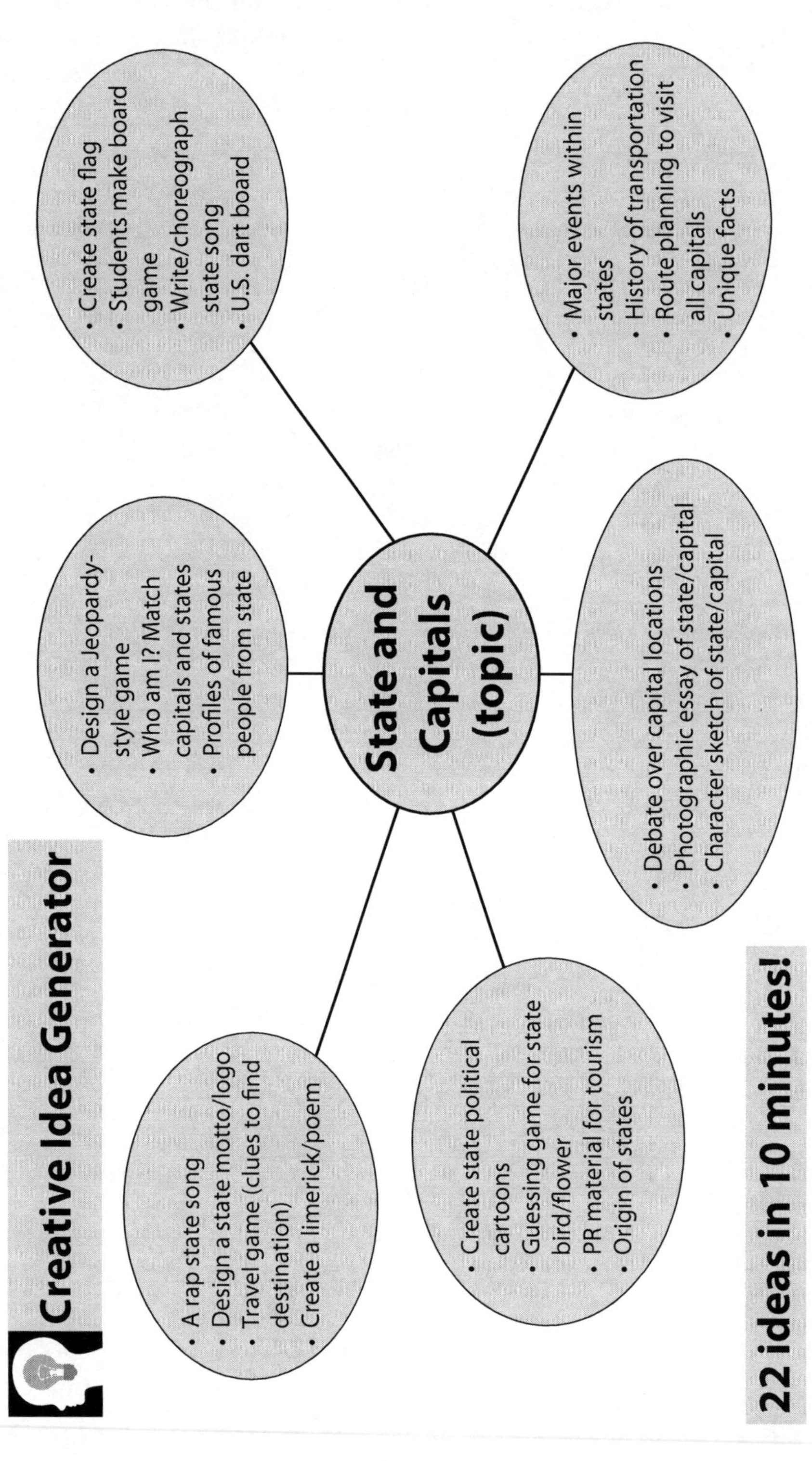

FIGURE D.1. Creative idea generator.

A NOTE ON PROBLEM-BASED LEARNING

Problem-based learning (PBL) has gained a good deal of attention for making the curriculum for students more engaging. We are a strong supporters of this approach to enhancing learning material in the regular (prescribed) curriculum. We do not, however, view it as creating the same experience as is the case with Type III Enrichment in the Triad Model. Generally speaking—and we know there are many variations on the use of PBL—teachers can use it to cover a standard curricular topic (e.g., Westward Expansion in U.S. history or social studies). There are expected outcomes that will probably show up on an end-of-unit test and perhaps even on a standardized achievement test. If the PBL approach makes the work more interesting and engaging, then such an approach has merit.

Type III Enrichment, however, is different because of the four requirements that make the problem more relevant to student interests and the investigative methods that students choose to select and pursue a topic of their own interest and methodology that further personalizes this approach to advanced level investigations or creative endeavors. The four requirements of a bona fide Type III Enrichment project are as follows:

1. personalization of interest (the student(s) selects the topic)
2. use of authentic methodology (involves some kind of original data gathering or creative expression)
3. no existing solution or "right" answer
4. designed to have an impact on an audience other than or in addition to the teacher

SUMMARY

Someone once asked us what is the "value" of infusing these activities into the curriculum? We answered, "High engagement and involvement activities are remembered long after the facts, or dates, or formulas you learned in fourth period math or social studies are forgotten." An infusion-based approach to education and learning allows teachers to find resources within the school, community, classroom, and in the people who reside within the community that will enable them to select highly engaging enrichment-based activities related to particular topics, inject them into the curriculum to make the topics more interesting, and provide support and encouragement for individuals and small groups who would like to extend their pursuit of enrichment activities. The Schoolwide Enrichment Model provides a framework to enrich the learning opportunities for students within a classroom where state standards or the

CCSS are present and must be addressed and incorporated into the lessons. By infusing prescribed standards with the richness of what lies beyond the standards or textbook, the academic and creative experiences of students become three-dimensional, as they recognize that the world is much bigger, and much more exciting than they could have ever imagined.

We began this chapter with a quote by Nancie Atwell, the winner of the Global Teacher of the Year Award, considered by many to be the Nobel Prize for educators. We end with her comment at the award ceremony about the importance of infusion.

> Teachers are people who can't imagine doing anything else; it's their passion. If there's nothing else you can ever imagine yourself doing, be a teacher. If you're passionate about making a difference in this world, be a teacher. A passionate teacher will find ways to infuse creativity and fun into learning, even amid the demands of testing and curriculum. But if the thought of teaching doesn't light you up—if you think it's just a job—don't go into education. There are more than enough teachers like that already. Am I trying to discourage my students from becoming educators? No. But I don't want to encourage someone to pursue a teaching career if the thought of working with children, teaching from the heart and the intellect, and making a difference in the lives of others doesn't light them up. No matter how bright a student is, no matter the GPA, we don't need people entering the field who aren't on fire. Because frankly, it's that fire that often lights our way when the horizon grows dark and ominous.

REFERENCES

Dotterer, A. M., & Lowe, K. (2011). Classroom context, school engagement, and academic achievement in early adolescence. *Journal of Youth and Adolescence, 40,* 1649–1660.

Greenwood, C. R. (1991). Longitudinal analysis of time, engagement, and achievement in at-risk versus non-risk students. *Exceptional Children, 57,* 521–535.

Maker, C. J., & Schiever, S. W. (2005). *Teaching models in education of the gifted* (3rd ed.). Austin, TX: Pro-Ed.

Reyes, M. R., Brackett, M. A., Rivers, S. E., White, M., & Salovey, P. (2012). Classroom emotional climate, student engagement, and academic achievement. *Journal of Educational Psychology, 104,* 700–712.

Smith, K., & Terry, G. (2014). *Global explorations–A multisensory, multicultural experience* (Unpublished curriculum unit). Charlotte: University of North Carolina at Charlotte.

Wang, M.-T., & Holcombe, R. (2010). Adolescents' perceptions of school environment, engagement, and academic achievement in middle school. *American Educational Research Journal, 47,* 633–662.

APPENDIX E
Student Product Assessment Form (SPAF)[1]

Joseph S. Renzulli and Sally M. Reis

RATIONALE UNDERLYING THIS ASSESSMENT FORM

The purpose of this form is to guide your judgment in the qualitative assessment of various types of products developed by students in enrichment programs. In using the instrument, three major considerations should always be kept in mind. First, the evaluation of more complex and creative types of products is always a function of human judgment. We do not think in terms of percentiles or standard scores when we evaluate paintings, architectural designs, or the usefulness of a labor-saving device. We must consider these products in terms of our own values and certain characteristics that indicate the quality, aesthetics, utility, and function of the overall contribution. In other words, we must trust our own judgment and learn to rely upon our guided subjective opinions when making assessments about complex products.

A second consideration relates to the individual worth of the product as a function of the student's age/grade level and experiential background. For example, a research project that reflects an advanced-level investigation and subsequent product by a first grader might not be considered an equally advanced level of involvement on the part of a sixth grader. Similarly, the work of a youngster from a disadvantaged background must be considered in light of the student's overall educational experiences, opportunities, and availability of advanced-level resource persons, materials, and equipment.

The third consideration relates to the most important purpose of any evaluation— student growth and improvement. This assessment instrument should be used to guide students toward excellence and therefore we strongly believe that it should be shared and discussed with students before the product is started. In other words, we believe the instrument should be reviewed with students during the early planning stages of the product. Students should have the opportunity to know and fully understand on what basis their final products will be assessed.

1 *Note*. From *The Schoolwide Enrichment Model: A How-To Guide for Talent Development* (3rd ed., pp. 199–204), by J. S. Renzulli & S. M. Reis, 2014, Waco, TX: Prufrock Press. Copyright 2014 by Prufrock Press. Reprinted with permission.

INSTRUCTIONS FOR USING THE ASSESSMENT FORM

Although most of the items included in the form relate directly to characteristics of the final product, it will be helpful if you also have access to any planning devices that have been used in the development of the product. Such planning devices might consist of logs, contracts, management plans, proposals, or any other record-keeping system. A planning device can help you to determine if prestated objectives have been met by comparing statements of objectives from the planning device with the final product. If such a planning device has not been utilized or is unavailable, you may want to request that the student complete a form that will provide you with the necessary background information. It is recommended that some type of planning device accompany all products that are submitted for rating. If it can be arranged, you may also want to interview the student who completed the product.

In using the Student Product Assessment Form, it will sometimes be necessary for you to do some detective work! For example, in determining the diversity of resources, you may need to examine footnotes, bibliographies, or references and materials listed on the planning device. You may also want to have the student complete a self-evaluation form relating to the completed product. This form may help to assess task commitment and student interest.

The Student Product Assessment Form can be used in a variety of ways. Individual teachers, resource persons, or subject matter specialists can evaluate products independently or collectively as members of a team. When two or more persons evaluate the same product independently, the average rating for each scale item can be calculated and entered on the Summary Form. When used in a research setting or formal evaluation situation, it is recommended that products be independently evaluated by three raters. One of these ratings should be completed by the teacher under whose direction the product was developed. A second form should be completed by a person who has familiarity with the subject matter area of the product. For example, a high school science teacher might be asked to rate the work of an elementary grade student who has completed a science-related product. The third rater might be someone who is independent of the school system or program in which the work was carried out.

ITEM FORMAT

At first glance, the items on the assessment form may seem to be long and complicated, but they are actually quite concise. Each item represents a single characteristic that is designed to focus your attention. The items are divided into the following three related parts:

1. **The Key Concept.** This concept is always present first and is printed in large type. It should serve to focus your attention on the main idea or characteristic being evaluated.

2. **The Item Description.** Following the Key Concept are one or more descriptive statements about how the characteristic might be reflected in the student's product. These statements are listed under the Key Concept.
3. **Examples.** In order to help clarify the meanings of the items, an actual example of students' work is provided. The examples are intended to elaborate upon the meaning of both the Key Concept and the Item Description. The examples are presented following each item description.

Important Note: The last item (No. 9) deals with an overall assessment of the product. In this case we have chosen a somewhat different format and examples have not been provided. When completing the ratings for Item No. 9, you should consider the product as a whole (globally) rather than evaluating its separate components in an analytic fashion.

Some of the items may appear to be unusually long or "detailish" for a rating scale but our purpose here is to improve the clarity and thus interrater reliability for the respective items. After you have used the scales a few times, you will probably only need to read the Key Concepts and Item Descriptions in order to refresh your memory about the meaning of an item. Research has shown interrater reliability is improved when items are more descriptive and when brief examples are provided in order to help clarify any misunderstanding that may exist on the parts of different raters.

NONAPPLICABLE ITEMS

Because of the difficulty of developing a single instrument that will be universally applicable to all types of products, there will occasionally be instances when some of the items do not apply to specific products. For example, in a creative writing project (poem, play, story) either the Level of Resources (No. 3) or Diversity of Resources (No. 4) might not apply if the student is writing directly from his or her own experiences. It should be emphasized however, that the nonapplicable category should be used very rarely in most rating situations.

HOW TO RATE STUDENT PRODUCTS

1. Fill out the information requested at the top of the Summary Sheet that accompanies the Student Product Assessment Form. A separate Summary Sheet should be filled out for each product that is evaluated.
2. Review the nine items on the Student Product Assessment Form. This review will help to give you a "mindset" for the things you will be looking for as you examine each product.
3. Examine the product by first doing a "quick overview" of the entire piece of work. Then do a careful and detailed examination of the product. Check (√) pages or places that you might want to reexamine and jot down brief notes

and comments about any strengths, weaknesses, or questions that occur as you review the product.

4. Turn to the first item on the Student Product Assessment Form. Read the Key Concept, Item Description, and Example. Enter the number that best represents your assessment in the "Rating" column on the Summary Sheet. Enter only whole numbers. In other words, do not enter ratings of 3 1/2 or 2 1/4. On those rare occasions when you feel an item does not apply, please check the N/A column on the Summary Sheet. Please note that we have only included an N/A response option for Item 9a on the Overall Assessment.
5. Turn to the second item and repeat the above process. If you feel you cannot render a judgment immediately, skip the item and return to it at a later time. Upon completion of the assessment process, you should have entered a number (or a check in the N/A column) for all items on the Summary Sheet.
6. Any comments you would like to make about the product can be entered at the bottom of the Summary Sheet.

STUDENT PRODUCT ASSESSMENT FORM SUMMARY SHEET

Name(s): ______________________________ Date: ______________

District: __________________________ School: ________________

Teacher: ______________________________ Grade: ______ Sex: ______

Product (Title and/or Brief Description): ______________________

____

Number of Weeks Students Worked on Product: ________________

Factors	Rating*	Not Applicable
1. Early Statement of Purpose		
2. Problem Focusing		
3. Level of Resources		
4. Diversity of Resources		
5. Appropriateness of Resources		
6. Logic, Sequence, and Transition		
7. Action Orientation		
8. Audience		
9. Overall Assessment		
9A. Originality of the Idea		
9B. Achieved Objectives Stated in the Plan		
9C. Advanced Familiarity with the Subject		
9D. Quality Beyond Age/Grade Level		
9E. Care, Attention to Detail, etc.		
9F. Time, Effort, Energy		
9G. Original Contribution		

Comments:

Person completing this form: ______________________________

***Rating Scales:**

Factors 1–8:
5 = To a great extent
3 = Somewhat
1 = To a limited extent

Factors 9A–9G:
5 = Outstanding
4 = Above average
3 = Average
2 = Below average
1 = Poor

STUDENT PRODUCT ASSESSMENT FORM

1. **Early Statement of Purpose.** Is the purpose (theme, thesis, research question) readily apparent in the early stages of the student's product? In other words, did the student define the topic or problem in such a manner that a clear understanding about the nature of the product emerges shortly after a review of the material?

   For example, in a research project dealing with skunks of northwestern Connecticut completed by a first-grade student, the overall purpose and scope of the product were readily apparent after reading the introductory paragraphs.

5	4	3	2	1	N/A
To a great extent		Somewhat		To a limited extent	

2. **Problem Focusing.** Did the student focus or clearly define the topic so that it represents a relatively specific problem within a larger area of study?

   For example, a study of "Drama in Elizabethan England" would be more focused than "A Study of Drama."

5	4	3	2	1	N/A
To a great extent		Somewhat		To a limited extent	

3. **Level of Resources.** Is there evidence that the student used resource materials or equipment that are more advanced, technical, or complex than materials ordinarily used by students at this age/grade level?

   For example, a sixth-grade student utilized a nearby university library to locate information about the history of clowns in the 12th through 16th century in the major European countries.

5	4	3	2	1	N/A
To a great extent		Somewhat		To a limited extent	

4. **Diversity of Resources.** Has the student made an effort to use several different types of resource materials in the development of the product? Has the student used any of the following information sources in addition to the standard use

of encyclopedias: textbooks, record/statistic books, biographies, how-to books, periodicals, films and filmstrips, letters, phone calls, personal interviews, surveys or polls, catalogs, and/or others?

For example, a fourth-grade student interested in the weapons and vehicles used in World War II read several adult-level books on this subject that included biographies, autobiographies, periodicals, and record books. He also conducted oral history interviews with local veterans of World War II, previewed films and film strips about the period, and collected letters from elderly citizens sent to them from their sons stationed overseas.

5	4	3	2	1	N/A
To a great extent		Somewhat		To a limited extent	

5. **Appropriateness of Resources.** Did the student select appropriate reference materials, resource persons, or equipment for the topic or area of study?

   For example, a student who was interested in why so much food is thrown away in the school cafeteria had to contact state officials to learn about state requirements and regulations that govern what must and can be served in public school cafeterias. With the aid of her teacher, she also had to locate resource books on how to design, conduct, and analyze a survey.

5	4	3	2	1	N/A
To a great extent		Somewhat		To a limited extent	

6. **Logic, Sequence, and Transition.** Does the product reflect a logical sequence of steps or events that ordinarily would be followed when carrying out an investigation in this area of study? Are the ideas presented clearly and logically and is there a smooth transition from one idea or subtopic to another?

   For example, a student decided to investigate whether or not a section of his city needs a new fire station with a salaried staff rather than the present volunteer staff. First the student needed to research different methods of investigative reporting such as appropriate interview skills. Next the student conducted interviews with both salaried and volunteer fire station staff. He then needed to learn about methods of survey design and reporting in order to analyze local resident opposition or support for the new fire station. After other logical steps in his research were completed, his accumulated findings led him to interviews with the mayor and the board of safety in the city and then to several construction companies that specialized in bids on such buildings. His final product was an editorial in the local newspaper that reflected his research and conclusions.

5	4	3	2	1	N/A
To a great extent		Somewhat		To a limited extent	

7. **Action Orientation.** Is it clear that the major goal of this study was for purposes other than merely reporting on or reproducing existing information, ideas, or knowledge? In other words, the student's purpose is clearly directed toward some kind of action (e.g., teaching ways to improve bicycle safety, presenting a lecture on salt pond life); some type of literary or artistic product (e.g., poem, painting, costume design); a scientific device or research study (e.g., building a robot, measuring plant growth as a function of controlled heat, light and moisture); or some type of leadership or managerial endeavor (e.g., editing a newspaper, producing/directing a movie).

   For example, a student decided to study the history of his city. After an extensive investigation, the student realized that other history books had been written about the city. He found, instead, that no one had ever isolated specific spots of historical significance in the city that were easily located and accessible. He began this task and decided to focus his research on producing an original historical walking tour of the city.

5	4	3	2	1	N/A
To a great extent		Somewhat		To a limited extent	

8. **Audience.** Is an appropriate audience specified or readily apparent in the product or Management Plan?

   For example, the student who researched the history of his city to produce an original walking tour presented his tour to the city council and the mayor. They, in turn, adopted it as the official walking tour of the city. It was reproduced in the city newspaper and distributed by the local historical society, library, and given out to registered guests in the city's hotels and motels.

5	4	3	2	1	N/A
To a great extent		Somewhat		To a limited extent	

9. **Overall Assessment.** Considering the product as a whole, provide a general rating for each of the following factors and mark the space provided to the right of the item:

Scale

5 = Outstanding   4 = Above Average
3 = Average   2 = Below Average
1 = Poor

9A. Originality of the idea. _____
9B. Achieved objectives stated in plan. _____
9C. Reflects advanced familiarity with the subject matter for a youngster of this age/grade level. _____
9D. Reflects a level of quality beyond what is normally expected of a student of this age and grade. _____
9E. Reflects care, attention to detail, and overall pride on the part of the student. _____
9F. Reflects a commitment of time, effort, and energy. _____
9G. Reflects an original contribution for a youngster of this age/grade level. _____

About the Authors

Joseph Renzulli is a professor of educational psychology at the University of Connecticut, where he also has served as the director of the Renzulli Center For Creativity, Gifted Education, and Talent Development. His research has focused on the identification and development of creativity and giftedness in young people, and on curricular and organizational models for differentiated learning environments that contribute to total school improvement. A focus of his work has been on applying the pedagogy of gifted education to the improvement of learning for all students. Dr. Renzulli is a UConn Distinguished Professor and holds Honorary Doctor of Laws Degrees from McGill University and the University of Camilo José Cela in Spain. The American Psychological Association named Dr. Renzulli among the 25 most influential psychologists in the world, and in 2009 Dr. Renzulli received the Harold W. McGraw, Jr. Award for innovation in education, considered by many to be "the Nobel Prize" for educators.

Jen Foreman teaches in Allegheny College's Psychology Department and Education Program. She received her Ph.D. in educational psychology from the University of Connecticut in 2013 and her M.S. in instructional leadership from Robert Morris University in 2008. Previously, Jen was a research associate for the National Research Center on the Gifted and Talented and has completed program evaluations as an independent consultant. She taught English in Simferopol, Crimea and has also been a homeschooling parent. Her research interests include the role of teacher nominations in identification for gifted programming, enrichment-based curriculum interventions, character development and service learning, and the neurodiversity movement.

Laurel Brandon is a research specialist in educational psychology and conducts research on imagination, creativity, and innovation with the Renzulli Center for Creativity, Gifted Education, and Talent Development at the University of Connecticut. She received her M.A. in educational psychology from the University of Connecticut in 2013. She was a gifted specialist in elementary schools for 6 years and was recognized by parents for her commitment to students. She has presented professional development in gifted education for districts and at state and national conferences. In addition to her work with the Renzulli Center, Laurel's research interests include enrichment pedagogy, interest and talent development, and positive psychology.